Being a Dad Who Leads

John MacArthur

HARVEST HOUSE PUBLISHERS
EUGENE, OREGON

Cover by Koechel Peterson & Associates, Inc., Minneapolis, Minnesota

Cover photo © maigi / Shutterstock

BEING A DAD WHO LEADS

Copyright © 2014 by John MacArthur
Published by Harvest House Publishers
Eugene, Oregon 97402
www.harvesthousepublishers.com

Library of Congress Cataloging-in-Publication Data
    MacArthur, John, 1939-
    Being a dad who leads / John MacArthur.
       pages cm
    Includes bibliographical references.
    ISBN 978-0-7369-5931-5 (hardcover)
    ISBN 978-0-7369-5932-2 (eBook)
    1. Fathers—Religious life. 2. Fatherhood—Religious aspects—Christianity. 3. Leadership—Religious aspects—Christianity. I. Title.
    BV4529.17.M25 2014
    248.8'421—dc23

                    2013034395

Printed in China

    14 15 16 17 18 19 20 21 22 / FC-JH / 10 9 8 7 6 5 4 3 2 1

To my children: Matt, Marcy, Mark, and Melinda.
All of them are walking with Christ,
raising their own children in the discipline
and instruction of the Lord.
That is far and away the greatest joy a father can experience.

Contents

Introduction

No duty in my life is more important or more sacred than my role as a husband and father. That is where my true character is most accurately seen, and it is the best single gauge of my overall success or failure as a leader and role model. Everything else I do as a pastor, educator, author, or ministry leader would be severely compromised if I failed to lead my own family properly. In fact, this is one of the key tests of whether any man is fit to lead the church, because "if a man does not know how to manage his own household, how will he take care of the church of God?" (1 Timothy 3:5). Conversely, if a man cultivates grace, godliness, and the mind of Christ in his home life, the fruit of the Spirit will naturally be seen in abundance throughout every facet of his life—his performance in the workplace, all his relationships, and his conduct in the world.

Furthermore, because home is where a person's true temperament is most clearly on display, no one knows the real character of a man better than his own children. They see with a keener clarity than most dads realize. If a man's public persona is merely a hypocritical veneer that disappears in the privacy of the home, the kids will be the first to see that. Indeed, it's hard to imagine anything more destructive to a child's moral and spiritual development. An ungodly, hypocritical, or indifferent dad is not only a constant, full-time negative role model; his influence also breeds cynicism, unbelief, discouragement, resentment, and a whole new generation of hypocrisy in his own children. Thus "the iniquity of the fathers [is visited] on the children to the third and the fourth generations" (Numbers 14:18; cf. Exodus 20:5; 34:7).

On the positive side, however, no one can have a more potent or longer-lasting influence for good in a child's life than a spiritually strong father. Bringing our children up "in the discipline and instruction of the Lord" (Ephesians 6:4) is not only a duty; it is also a great privilege, for "a wise son makes a father glad" (Proverbs 10:1; 15:20). There is no greater joy in life than to see one's own children walking in the truth (cf. 3 John 4). In other words, nothing is a more worthy investment of any father's time and energy than this: *Be a godly leader in your own home.* The returns you will reap include eternal riches of inestimable value, and the earthly rewards alone are sweeter and more valuable than any amount of material wealth.

This book, I trust, will be a help and encouragement to you as you pursue that goal. I have purposely kept it brief, simple, and focused. That is, after all, in keeping with the biblical instructions for fathers. Fatherhood is, of course, a prominent theme from Genesis to Revelation, and principles of parenting are scattered throughout. But glean and organize all of them together and what you will discover is that the Bible's guidelines for fathers are few and simple. Unlike many of today's parenting manuals, Scripture doesn't treat parenting as an arcane or bewildering conundrum. The father's duties are straightforward and fairly basic. What makes fatherhood *seem* difficult are our own inconsistencies and weaknesses. That's because parenting is first and foremost a spiritual task—one in which personal righteousness, self-control, and the mortification of our own flesh are all necessary prerequisites to proper discipline and instruction of our children. In short, the only way to be a dad who leads well is to be a dad who *lives* well.

May God bless you and empower you in your pursuit of that goal.

The responsibility given to the husband [to love his wife] should not be undertaken lightly. It is a call to shepherd, provide, protect, and lead. It requires love, self-sacrifice, humility, and diligence. Ultimately, it looks to heaven and purposes to live each day in light of that future inheritance. In the meantime, it rests in the grace of God—knowing that the best of human relationships can be fully enjoyed only in light of our fellowship with Him.[1]

RICH GREGORY

CHAPTER 1

The Starting Point of a Dad's Leadership

By God's design and God's will, the husband is the head of the household; he is the leader of the family. Scripture makes it clear he is the one responsible for the success of the marriage and family, and the well-being of everyone involved. This headship is affirmed from the beginning of time at creation, a fact explained by the apostle Paul in 1 Corinthians 11, where he states, "The man is the head of a woman...For man does not originate from woman, but woman from man; for indeed man was not created for the woman's sake, but woman for the man's sake" (verses 3,8-9). In that passage, Paul upholds the concept of a man's headship in the family by appealing to the order of creation—man was created first, then woman—and the fact woman was created to help the man (Genesis 2:18,21-24).

Later, in the most significant passage on marriage and family relationships in the entire New Testament, Paul once again addresses the married man's role as head of his own home. In the course of writing about the relationships between husbands, wives, and children in Ephesians 5:22–6:4, Paul establishes that God's design is that "the husband is the head of the wife, as Christ also is the head of the church" (verse 23). He then goes on to provide specific instruction on how husbands are to fulfill their leadership role, beginning with this important command: "Husbands, love your wives, just as Christ also loved the church" (verse 25).

This, then, is the husband's supreme responsibility—loving his wife. Using Christ's love for the church as his example, Paul explains in the subsequent verses how the husband's love is to be manifest. Every man is to love his wife with a sacrificial, purifying, caring, unbreakable, Christlike love—all of which we will explore as we continue through this chapter.

A Lack of Male Leadership in the Home

Yet the questions being asked by many today are these: Where are the strong husbands? Where are the loyal, loving, leading husbands and fathers? Where are the men who are willing to stand as the backbone, the solid framework or structure on which you can build a marriage and a family—and, in turn, a society?

Too many men today live in worlds completely isolated from their families. Outside the home, they are aggressive doers and problem solvers who come up with all sorts of innovative ways to make money and obtain promotions, prestige, and respect from the people in their outside world. Yet in the home, for the most part, they are passive, indifferent, and irresponsible. Though they may be present in the home, they are not actively engaged in the everyday dynamics of family life.

Looking at the problem from a historical-sociological perspective, one writer gave this observation:

> A series of historical events, beginning at the Industrial Revolution, traversing the search for American independence and the Second Great Awakening, and culminating in Victorianism, has had the net result of disestablishing American men from a true role of fatherhood and moral leadership in our land. The American male, at one time the ever-present guide of the close-knit colonial family, left his family for the factory and the materialistic lure that the Industrial Revolution brought. The most numerous and most active members of the church, the men—who commonly debated theology in the colonial marketplace—were, in time, to be found arguing business practices in the tavern. The fathers who labored hard to instill the value of cooperation in their offspring, in time gave their children the example of unlimited individual competition. Men who once taught their children respect and obedience toward godly authority came to act as though independence were a national virtue. Men who once had an active hand in the education of their sons relegated this responsibility to a public school system…

> Over the course of 150 years, from the mid-eighteenth century to the end of the nineteenth century, American men walked out on their God-given responsibility for moral and spiritual leadership in the homes, schools, and Sunday schools of the nation. As sociologist Lawrence Fuchs notes, "The

groundwork for the 20th-century fatherless home was set. By the end of the 19th century for the first time it was socially and morally acceptable for men not to be involved with their families."[2]

What you have here is the disappearance of the American husband and father—all for what was initially a noble purpose—to provide a better life for his family. But soon the father was operating in a realm completely independent of his own family, a world his family knew little about, if anything. This has brought about both subtle and not-so-subtle changes that have had a devastating impact on the family.

For a variety of reasons, many men today are not actively involved in their family life. They've got work to do; they're too tired when they get home; they need to work on the car, play golf with the guys, work out at the gym. Thus they don't have time to interact and play with the kids, go to their games, and attend their school programs.

Now, we can look at this historical-sociological explanation for what has happened to fathers and say these changes had their roots in the Industrial Revolution, which basically created a world outside of the home. And there are those who would say there's not much that can be done about it—we'll just have to do the best we can with this reality.

But that is only part of the picture. It is merely one of many factors that have diminished the amount of time fathers are available in the home. There are other reasons as well, and many of them simply come down to the fact the father is making choices in his life that pull him away from his family. Yes, there are instances when circumstances may make it difficult for a father to be available in the home. But if we're honest with ourselves, it's frequently a matter of how a man decides to prioritize his time.

The end result is that many men are not fulfilling their biblical calling in the home. They haven't made home life enough of a priority that they commit themselves to their most basic obligations as a husband and father. The Bible says a man is responsible to lead in his home, care for his wife, and provide instruction for his children. Those responsibilities are clearly spelled out in Scripture. When they're neglected, the family will fall apart. In effect, men who abandon their God-given role in the home have forfeited true manhood. Marital discord and a chaotic home life are among the inevitable results.

Thankfully, there are still men who care about fulfilling their God-given role in the home, and the fact you are reading this book tells me you are one of them. My heart always rejoices when a father expresses a genuine desire to live as a godly leader and example to his wife and children—a desire like that expressed in the letter below:

> Greetings John:
>
> My lovely wife and I have been married for seven years. We have two amazing young boys. They are sweet boys with loving hearts, so discipline thus far hasn't been too terribly hard. Here's my greatest concern, though—I want them to truly know the Lord. Am I properly shepherding their young hearts as their father, and is there more I can do?
>
> Every day I see how much they need me to be a strong man of God, especially in these times. I want

them to look at me and have no question in their minds who their daddy lines up after—that Jesus Christ is my Lord and Master.

I know I will make mistakes along the way, as I am but a man. But I want to give them my best, laying a solid foundation and sowing as many seeds as possible. I would appreciate your advice as a Bible teacher and a dad of boys. I know I will be able to teach my sons high and lofty truths of Scripture when they are older, and I am so looking forward to those days. But these young days are priceless and I don't want to miss out on good teaching moments about our great God. Thank you, brother, for any help and encouragement you have for me.

The Priority of a Husband and Father

If we're ever going to restore family life to God's design, it starts with the husband's leadership in the home. This means moral and spiritual leadership, as well as emotional and physical security. That's where it all begins; that's what male headship is all about. It doesn't involve some sort of mystical search for one's "inner manhood," nor is it something that has to be figured out through psychological or sociological analysis. Rather, it's based on being diligent to apply straightforward and practical principles found in the Bible.

If you're a Christian man, surely you recognize that success in your home life is far more important than success in your career. That's especially true when you consider what kind of testimony your home life is to the people in your workplace.

Neglect the care of your family, and you'll lose credibility in the outside world when it comes to anything that has to do with the Christian faith.

Biblically speaking, your responsibilities as a husband and father come before everything else. That's how it was designed by God, who created the marriage union and the family unit as the earliest and most foundational elements of all human society. When the family breaks down, society breaks down as well. A strong family—and a healthy society—starts with the husband's leadership in the home.

So what does this leadership look like? How does a Christian man fulfill God's calling for him to lead in the home? More specifically, how can he lead his wife and children in a way that strengthens family unity, blesses those outside the home, and brings glory to God?

In Ephesians 5:25-31, God lays out the husband's responsibilities to his wife, and a little later in Ephesians 6:4, we find His divine instruction for how fathers are to lead their children. This is where we will focus our attention in the first part of this book.

Leading by Loving Your Wife

When Paul described the Christian husband's responsibilities to his wife, here's what the apostle wrote:

> Husbands, love your wives, just as Christ also loved the church and gave Himself up for her, so that He might sanctify her, having cleansed her by the washing of water with the word, that He might present to Himself the church in all her glory, having no spot or

wrinkle or any such thing; but that she would be holy
and blameless. So husbands ought also to love their
own wives as their own bodies. He who loves his own
wife loves himself; for no one ever hated his own
flesh, but nourishes and cherishes it, just as Christ
also does the church, because we are members of His
body. For this reason a man shall leave his father and
mother and shall be joined to his wife, and the two
shall become one flesh (Ephesians 5:25-31).

Note where it all begins—with the command, "Husbands,
love your wives" (verse 25). Three verses later it's repeated again:
"Husbands ought also to love their own wives." In fact, love
is the theme of this entire pas-
sage—a man's love for his wife,
and Christ's love for the church.
This makes it pretty clear that a
married man's supreme responsibility is love for his wife. That

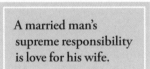

A married man's
supreme responsibility
is love for his wife.

comes first. Everything else in life flows out from that.

If Paul hadn't illustrated how this love is to be shown, we
would probably run off in a thousand different directions trying to figure out what it means for a man to show love to his
wife. Our world today has such mixed-up ideas about love—
ideas that are far removed from the biblical definition of love.
Musicians have written endlessly about love and the struggles
people experience in relationships. Love is usually defined as
an emotion that comes and goes, rises and falls, ebbs and flows.
It's described as a feeling that causes people to do things they
ordinarily wouldn't do. Love as portrayed in popular music

and secular lore is not a sacrifice, a commitment, or a choice you make, but something that *happens to you*—you fall into it, or it sweeps you off your feet. People talk about waiting for love to come to them. They nurture romantic expectations about love that are untenable and unrealistic. They think of love in terms of what it will give them instead of what authentic love requires. Virtually all the popular notions about love fostered by our entertainment-saturated, self-centered culture fall far short of the real thing.

Thankfully, Paul doesn't leave husbands in the dark about how they are to love their wives. He cuts to the central issue in as few words as possible. He is very clear and specific, saying that a husband should love his wife "just as Christ also loved the church and gave Himself up for her" (verse 25).

Christ's love for the church is the model husbands are to follow in their relationship with their wives. In other words, a husband's love for his wife is supposed to be a living illustration of the redemptive love of Christ. Christ's love is the eternal standard and archetype. The love of a husband for his wife is meant to be a close facsimile. This explains the sacredness of the marriage union—especially the unique significance of the husband's calling. The role and duties of earthly husbands are designed by God specifically to illustrate the heavenly Bridegroom's timeless love for His church. That love is described for us in Ephesians 5:25-30, and we find that it manifests itself in four key ways.

Loving Your Wife with a Sacrificial Love

We begin with Ephesians 5:25, which says, "Husbands,

love your wives, just as Christ also loved the church and gave Himself up for her." What did Christ do for the church? He sacrificed Himself for her. He died on the cross for unworthy sinners who collectively constitute His chosen bride. His love for them was completely undeserved, and it was given freely, by *His* initiative—not because of any merit in those whom he loves; not owing to any inherent charm or appeal they might possess; and not because of any advantage or benefit they give Him in return. His love for them is not a reward they earn; it is purely a sacrifice He makes on their behalf. That is the standard husbands are to follow.

In Acts 20:28, we read that Christ purchased the church "with His own blood." Romans 5:8 pictures Jesus pouring out His love in His death for us. In Romans 8:38-39, we are told it is an undying, unchanging love—He loves us with a love from which we can never be separated.

In response to the command made to husbands in Ephesians 5:25 the great Victorian preacher C.H. Spurgeon said this:

> A husband loves his wife with a constant love, and so does Christ his church. He will not cast her away tomorrow having loved her today. He does not vary in his affection. He may change in his display of affection, but the affection itself is still the same. A husband loves his wife with an enduring love; it never will die out. He says, "Till death us do part will I cherish thee"; but Christ will not even let death part his love to his people. "Nothing shall separate us from the love of God which is in Christ Jesus our

Lord." A husband loves his wife with a hearty love, with a love that is true and intense. It is not mere lip service. He does not merely speak, but he acts; he is ready to provide for her wants; he will defend her character; he will vindicate her honor; because his heart is set upon her. It is not merely with the eye that he delights now and then to glance upon her, but his soul has her continually in his remembrance—she has a mansion in his heart from which she can never be cast away. She has become a portion of himself; she is a member of his body, she is part of his flesh and of his bones; and so is the church to Christ forever, an eternal spouse.[3]

That's a pretty remarkable love, isn't it? The great challenge of a husband loving his wife in the same way that Christ loved the church is that there is always room to grow. Christ's love is a perfect and eternal love, and husbands are called to emulate it. Christ loved us even when we were rebellious sinners who had utterly rejected Him. He died on the cross for us, showing a self-sacrificial love that expected nothing in return, a love that cost His life. That's the kind of love He poured out for the church, and that's the kind of love husbands are called to have for their wives.

Every now and then you'll hear a husband say, "I love my wife too much." But does he love her as much as Christ loved the church? If not, then he doesn't love her enough. Christ's love for the church is the standard by which husbands should measure their love for their wives, and let's face it squarely: We all fall short. Given the clarity and force of this command, no husband has any right to feel smug. Notice: Scripture doesn't adjust the standard to compensate for our weakness. It may sound like hyperbole, but it's not. Husbands are commanded to *give themselves up* for their wives, and the singular example we are given to follow is the infinite self-sacrifice Christ made to redeem sinners. In other words, there's no possibility of loving and sacrificing "too much."

The apostle Peter speaks of sacrificial love as well when he says, "Husbands…live with your wives in an understanding way, as with someone weaker, since she is a woman; and show her honor as a fellow heir of the grace of life, so that your prayers will not be hindered" (1 Peter 3:7). We see here in very practical terms how a husband is to love his wife, and we can break this down into three parts:

1. Consideration

"Live with your wives in an understanding way." That is, show sensitivity to her. Take the time to meet her needs and understand what she is thinking. Ask her about her concerns, goals, dreams, affections, and desires. Very simply, take time to listen to her. Before you can express a sacrificial love for her—the kind that meets her needs—you need to know what those needs are.

2. Chivalry

Peter graciously reminds us that our wife is "someone weaker, since she is a woman." People today might think this is a demeaning statement, but it's not. Peter was simply pointing out that a woman doesn't have the same kind of physical strength as a man, and therefore she needs his protection.

Though your wife is fully your equal from a spiritual stand-point (Galatians 3:28), she is physically weaker and in need of your provision and strength. To provide that for her is to love her.

3. Communion

Your wife is "a fellow heir of the grace of life." She is your spiritual equal. As such, you are to cultivate companionship and fellowship with her, not lord it over her. This was a foreign concept to the Greco-Roman culture of Peter's day. Husbands were generally uninterested in friendship with their wives, expecting them to merely take care of the house and bear children. In contrast, the Christian husband is to cultivate a loving and intimate companionship with his wife, which is one of the richest blessings he can know in this life.

In these ways, 1 Peter 3:7 defines for us all the more what a sacrificial love looks like. Ultimately, the Christian husband loves his wife *not* for what she can do for him, but because of what he desires to do for her. That's how Christ's love works. He loves us not because there's something in us that attracts Him to us; He loves us because He determined to love us in spite of our unattractiveness. He loves us with a sympathetic love that seeks to understand us, assist us, comfort and equip us, and meet our needs. It's a love we don't deserve, a love that will never end. It's a love that perseveres even when we fail Him. That's the kind of love you as a husband are to have for your wife.

Loving Your Wife with a Purifying Love

Second, Christ's love for the church is a purifying love.

Ephesians 5:25-28 says that Christ "gave Himself up" for the church "so that He might sanctify her, having cleansed her by the washing of water with the word, that He might present to Himself the church in all her glory, having no spot or wrinkle or any such thing; but that she would be holy and blameless."

Paul is speaking here about a spiritually uplifting love, a spiritually beneficial love. You are to love your wife in such a way that you encourage her toward greater godliness. Such love leads a woman to become more holy and allows her full beauty to shine. We see here that the truest, finest, and most enduring beauty of a woman is not external; rather, it is internal. It is holiness that makes her genuinely beautiful, putting on display the work of God in her heart. First Samuel 16:7 contrasts outer and inner beauty when it says, "Man looks at the outward appearance, but the LORD looks at the heart." Women are therefore exhorted not to be so concerned with decorations that enhance their physical charms but to beautify the inner person. In 1 Peter 3:3-4 they are told: "Your adornment must not be merely external…but let it be the hidden person of the heart."

For that reason, one of the best ways you as a husband can show love to your wife is by leading her to ever-increasing virtue. Encourage her toward holiness in the same way Christ seeks to sanctify the church so that "He might present to Himself the church in all her glory, having no spot or wrinkle or any such thing" (Ephesians 5:27). Christ's supreme desire for the church is to present her in all her glorious splendor without spot or stain.

Ephesians 5:26 tells us this cleansing takes place "by the washing of water with the Word." In other words, God's Word has a purifying effect on our lives. Psalm 119:9 tells us that if we want to keep our way pure, we are to live according to His Word. So you as a husband are to ensure your wife is continually exposed to God's Word so that she might remain holy and blameless. That can include hearing the preaching of Scripture during Sunday worship, getting involved in a Bible study, and encouraging her to read books or listen to messages that provide solid biblical instruction.

This also means you don't lead your wife into sin or expose her to iniquity. Don't speak or act in ways that might embitter her or cause her to become angry or hostile. Don't intentionally prod her in ways that would cause her to respond in a sinful manner. If you really love your wife, you're going to hate anything that defiles her. You're going to do all you can to protect and preserve her purity. The loving husband, like Christ, seeks only to present his bride glorious and exalted. He seeks to honor her. This is a fundamental element of your role as the spiritual leader of the home.

Loving Your Wife with a Caring Love

Third, Paul says that a husband's love for his wife is to be a caring love: "Husbands ought also to love their own wives as their own bodies. He who loves his own wife loves himself" (Ephesians 5:28).

What exactly does it mean to love your wife as your own body? Paul is presenting a simple concept here: We are usually pretty good about taking care of our own bodies. When we're sick, we rest and do what's necessary to get better. When we're hungry, we eat. When we're thirsty, we satisfy our thirst. When we're sweaty or dirty, we wash ourselves off. When it comes to feeding ourselves, clothing ourselves, or making ourselves comfortable, we're usually quite self-motivated. We're quick to take care of our own needs. And Paul is saying we're to treat our wives with the same level of attention we devote to ourselves.

The next few verses then bring us to a crucial point: "For no one ever hated his own flesh, but nourishes and cherishes it, just as Christ also does the church, because we are members of His body" (verses 29-30). When you married your wife, the two of you became one flesh. That's why Paul then writes, "For this reason a man shall leave his father and mother and shall be joined to his wife, and the two shall become one flesh" (verse 31). In the marriage relationship, you and your wife are one. And in salvation, your wife is one with Christ. So in a very real sense, the way you treat your wife is the way you are treating Christ. If you don't love your wife in a caring way, then you aren't caring for yourself and you don't love Christ as you should.

> If you want your marriage to be blessed, you need to take care of your wife.

If you want your marriage to be blessed, you need to take care of your wife. When you know she has a need, you should seek to meet it. When you know she has a longing in her heart and it's a reasonable one that will add to her virtue and well-being, you ought to do what you can to fulfill it. Your wife is a God-given treasure to be cared for, nourished, and protected. That's exactly how Christ takes care of His church.

Looking again at Ephesians 5:29, note the two terms "nourishes" and "cherishes." In the original Greek text, the word "nourishes" is a term used primarily to speak of bringing up children. It's the same word Paul uses a little later in Ephesians 6:4: "Fathers...bring [your children] up in the discipline and instruction of the Lord." Typically we think in terms of nourishing our children, but in Ephesians 5:29, Paul says we are to nourish or care for our wives. As a husband, you are responsible to nurture your wife so that she, in turn, can effectively nurture the children in her God-given role as their mother.

Next, the Greek word translated "cherishes" means "to warm with body heat." It's sometimes translated "to melt." It is used of a mother bird who coaxes her children to draw closer to her so she can keep them warm and secure. In the context of husbands, Ephesians 5:29 is saying we're to support and care for our wives in a way that makes them feel loved and secure. It's a challenge to do this in a world that teaches women to be tough and independent. And it takes a tremendous amount of spiritual leadership from a man to provide his wife with warmth, strength, and security. As a husband, that's your responsibility.

The Husband as a Provider

Going back to the analogy that you as a husband are to love your wife just as Christ loved the church—have you ever noticed that it's Christ who does all the providing? It is He who nourishes, protects, and preserves. Nothing is said about the church giving back to Christ. In the same way, your love for your wife is to be a providing love. Christ didn't love the church with the expectation of getting something back in return, and that's the kind of love you're to have as a husband. Just as Christ is the provider for His church, you are to be the provider for your wife.

At this point you might be saying, "Well, I'd have to sacrifice my career to do that." Then sacrifice your career. Or let go of whatever else it is that's keeping you from loving your wife as you should. Maybe you won't get promoted as high or often as you would like. Or maybe you won't have opportunity to pursue some of your own personal goals or pleasures as much. But in the end, you're going to be so richly rewarded by the bliss of living according to God's design for marriage that you'll find it well worth anything you've had to give up.

The Difficulty of Being a Provider

Scripture makes it clear that from the beginning, God's design has been for the husband to be the provider. Yet this role was made more difficult when Adam and Eve fell into sin. Remember the curse God pronounced as a result of their disobedience? God told Eve she would know pain in childbirth. Then He told Adam, "Cursed is the ground because of you; in toil you will eat of it all the days of your life…By the sweat of your face you will eat bread" (Genesis 3:17,19). In other words, from here onward, the task of being a provider would require hard labor. The curse was a direct hit on the man's responsibility to provide, as well as a direct hit on the woman's responsibility to bear children.

This tells us that the husband's work of being a provider won't be easy. In fact, it's so difficult that it can only be fulfilled in the power of the Spirit and a transformed life. As Ephesians 5:30 says, if you are a Christian, you are a member of Christ's body. You are one with Christ, and the Spirit dwells in you. And as you walk in the power of the Spirit and yield to His

Word and His control, you will be able to care for your wife in the same way Christ cares for His church.

Loving Your Wife with an Unbreakable Love

The fourth characteristic of a husband's love for his wife is that it is to be an unbreakable love. In Ephesians 5:31, Paul quoted from Genesis 2:24 and wrote, "For this reason a man shall leave his father and mother and shall be joined to his wife, and the two shall become one flesh." Marriage is the coming together of a man and a woman who leave their parents and create a new union with a unique identity all its own. It is two lives becoming one.

What is meant by the phrase "one flesh"? The primary reference is to the sexual union between the husband and wife, which is the most obvious evidence that the two have become one. This enables them to give birth to children who carry genetic traits from both of them, which makes the children an emblem of the oneness between a husband and wife.

Yet there's far more to the concept of a one-flesh relationship than that. In 1 Corinthians 6:15, Paul wrote, "Do you not know that your bodies are members of Christ?" The believer's union with Christ is of course *spiritual*, not physical. Yet the apostle expressly says that in such a union even the physical bodies of Christians essentially become "members of Christ"—one body. As a matter of fact, he goes on to say that any sexual sin by a believer is a desecration of Christ: "Shall I then take away the members of Christ and make them members of a prostitute? May it never be! Or do you not know that the one who joins himself to a prostitute is one body with her? For He says, 'The two shall become one flesh'" (verses

15-16). Obviously, then, the ideas of spiritual union and physical intimacy are inextricably linked. This suggests that the phrase "one flesh" has to do with much more than just sexual intimacy.

Indeed, marriage is a merger between two souls, not merely the joining of two bodies. The physical union illustrates and exemplifies the fuller reality of what marriage means, but by no means does it exhaust the significance of two becoming one. Marriage as God designed it not only brings two people together in physical intimacy; it also binds the couple's hearts and minds together. Its full reality entails a spiritual union that engulfs every aspect of life.

When a man and woman become one in marriage, they enter into a unique, intimate, and comprehensive personal relationship. Their whole identity is redefined. They give up their personal autonomy (and every independent or self-focused aspect of their individual identity), because they are now one with another person. Nothing of value is actually lost in the union; both individuals gain immeasurably from being joined with each other. And "what therefore God has joined together, let no man separate" (Matthew 19:6). That's why God hates divorce—because it severs what is designed to be an indissoluble, indivisible, one-flesh relationship (Malachi 2:16).

A Permanent Union

Ephesians 5:31 quotes directly from Genesis 2:24. The King James Version's rendering of that verse is familiar, because it is commonly quoted in traditional wedding ceremonies: "Therefore shall a man leave his father and his mother, and shall cleave unto his wife: and they shall be one flesh." Jesus quotes that same verse from Genesis in Matthew 19:5. The old English word "cleave" speaks of the permanence of the marriage union. It's the Greek word *proskollao*, which means "to be glued or cemented together; to hold fast." A husband and wife are to stick together in a union that is not only physical but also includes oneness of mind, oneness of heart, and oneness of purpose. In the marriage union, they are brought together in a magnificent, personal intimacy that is unlike any other kind of earthly relationship.

A Forgiving Union

All through my years in ministry, I've heard women who have said, "I want to keep my marriage together, but it's difficult to live with this guy." And I've heard men say, "I want to stay married, but I don't know if I can live any longer with this woman."

If a marriage has gotten to that point, it's frequently because the husband, wife, or both have ceased to practice forgiveness in their relationship. When one or both spouses are continually unforgiving, the frustration toward each other accumulates, and that, in turn, will increasingly strain the relationship.

But consider this: How often has the Lord forgiven you? How about every day? His love for you will never change. Even when you succumb to temptation and fall into sin, you are still His chosen bride. And when you confess your sins, "He is faithful and righteous to forgive us our sins and to cleanse us from all unrighteousness" (1 John 1:9). Nothing will ever separate you from Christ's love (Romans 8:38-39).

It is that kind of loving, gracious forgiveness that we are

to practice in the marriage relationship. Ephesians 4:32 commands us to "be kind to one another, tender-hearted, forgiving each other, just as God in Christ also has forgiven you." We who have been forgiven so much by God ought to be more than willing to forgive the relatively lesser offenses of others—especially our wives.

With that in mind, how often are we to forgive one another? Jesus said "seventy times seven" (Matthew 18:22)—His point being that we should *always* be willing to forgive, without limit. You are called to love your wife with an unbreakable love that keeps forgiving no matter what. In marriage, you are one flesh for life. Can a man cast off his wife? Let me answer that with another question: Can Christ cast off His church?

The Key to Real Marital Bliss

In Ephesians 5:25-31, we see that a husband is to love his wife with a sacrificial love, a purifying love, a caring love, and an unbreakable love. And the role model for that love is the Lord Jesus Christ Himself. That brings us to this important point: The marriage union between a Christian man and a Christian woman is a picture of the union between Christ and His church. That is why we're to treat the marriage relationship with great reverence—it is a sacred symbol of Christ's relationship to His church. God meant for marriage to be a permanent and unbreakable union that speaks volumes to the world about the love Christ has for His church.

Yet no husband can show such Christlike love for his wife apart from the power of the Spirit. As we walk in the Spirit (Galatians 5:16)—meaning we humbly yield to the Spirit, trusting Him to empower us to live in obedience to the commands of Scripture—we manifest the fruit of the Spirit, which includes love, joy, peace, patience, kindness, goodness, faithfulness, gentleness, and self-control (verses 22-23). As you live under the Spirit's control and commit yourself to humbly living out God's Word, you will be empowered to love your wife in the way God has called you to. You will experience the lasting romance and joy in your marriage that so many other people have found elusive.

As you lead in love and cherish your wife in the same way that Christ loved the church, your marriage relationship will come to know the fullness of all that God intended for it to be. It is as you fulfill your role as a loving leader in your home that your marriage will blossom and your wife will delight in fulfilling her role in the relationship. And when your children see that their father and mother are committed to living out God's design for marriage, they'll experience the stability and security that come from a healthy home environment. They'll be richly blessed, and God will receive honor and glory as people around you see His perfect plan for husbands and wives lived out.

We should give our children the impression that the most wonderful thing in the world is Christianity; and that there is nothing in life comparable to being a Christian.[4]

MARTYN-LLOYD JONES

CHAPTER 2

Raising Your Children in the Lord, Part 1

When you consider the enormous amount of work that is involved in raising a child from birth to adulthood, it would be easy to assume that perhaps the Bible would provide a lengthy set of instructions about how to parent effectively. After all, thousands of books have been written on parenting. There are numerous media programs and ministries dedicated to providing guidance on marriage and family life. There are an endless number of experts who offer advice on parenting methods that, if followed, are claimed to produce a happy family. And yet many of the parenting trends and techniques that are popular today will quickly be replaced by a whole new set of trends and techniques tomorrow. All this can leave parents feeling overwhelmed as they try to keep up with what popular culture says they are to do for their children.

But when we look to the New Testament, we find that the one passage that goes into the greatest depth about God's pattern for marriage and family life offers a remarkably simple exhortation for parents. In fact, the apostle Paul summarized the essence of all our parenting efforts in just one statement: "Fathers, do not provoke your children to anger, but bring them up in the discipline and instruction of the Lord" (Ephesians 6:4).

Don't let the simplicity of that statement fool you. As we will soon see, it aims at the very heart of all that we need to know about raising children. While there are certainly other common-sense parenting principles that we as parents might find useful for training up our children, this one instruction provides a master guideline for everything that we do as parents. Every aspect of our children's development is affected by how carefully and faithfully we apply Ephesians 6:4 to their lives.

That's not to say parenting is a simple task—it's not. It's a serious and challenging responsibility. It requires a lot of time and personal sacrifice, and there are significant costs involved. When our children are little, they require constant attention and care. As they grow older and more independent, they still need our oversight and involvement in their education and activities. For example, we need to provide them with guidance regarding spiritual matters, choosing the right peers, using their finances wisely, and growing into adulthood.

The Two Great Pressures Parents Face

Our responsibilities as parents are made even more difficult by two great challenges before us. Because these challenges are so pervasive, we'll want to take a closer look at them before we begin our study of Ephesians 6:4.

The External Pressure of Culture

The first pressure we as parents face is external—it's brought upon our families by the culture around us. There was a time when life was largely centered in the home and the outside world had a rather minimal impact on children. That's not true anymore.

It used to be that families spent a lot of their time together. Most of their activities revolved around the home. Meals, activities, and participation in church and school life were largely done together. Parents were the predominant influence in their children's lives. They were the main source of input and were able to wield control over how much exposure children had to the outside world. They made sure that what a child learned was appropriate for the child's age and capacity to deal with certain issues. In other words, children had controlled exposure, and that was a good thing.

Yet that's not how it is today. Neil Postman, the late professor and department chair of communication arts at New York University, wrote about this in his book *The Disappearance of Childhood*.[5] The thesis Postman set forth is the idea that childhood, as a unique period of human development, is disappearing.

Among Postman's observations, for example, is that clothing used to be different for children. Now it is as much like adults as possible. Kids want to copy the fashions and fads they see their parents and other adults wearing.

Childhood games have changed as well. It used to be kids would invent their own games and play them together. Kids played just for the fun of it, and their games were usually the expression of wonderful childhood imagination.

But that has changed. For example, many of today's childhood sports games are copies of adult games, complete with structured organizations, special fees, and sophisticated equipment. Oftentimes these games are not so much for the fun of the kids, but for the egos of the parents, coaches, and other adults involved. And they cultivate a pervasive atmosphere of competitiveness that places great pressure on the kids to win and not just have fun.

Then there's the whole matter of electronic games, many of which consume enormous amounts of time and are expensive. Frequently these games are played solo, which means less interaction with other kids.

In the past, society used to hold to the view that children were to be protected. They were to be taught and cared for according to what was appropriate for their age. Information was provided to them in prescribed amounts that didn't expose them prematurely to knowledge they weren't equipped to handle. There were certain things withheld from children because they weren't ready for them.

But all that has changed—initially with radio and television, and even more so with the Internet and social media. Children are now exposed to all sorts of ideas and information without any regard to whether they can handle it. The best and worst of what society has to offer is all too readily available with easy access.

Postman, in *The Disappearance of Childhood*, observed that television is undifferentiated in its accessibility. That is, it doesn't make any distinctions between an adult and a child. The same is true about the Internet. Both television and the Internet have a pervasive influence on our children, exposing them to content that we as parents don't want them to see.

Children used to be unknowing and innocent when it came to certain issues in life. But that innocence has been lost in today's electronic environment. Kids are exposed to ideas and content their minds and emotions are not ready to handle. And under the onslaught of this corrupt world with its wrong concepts, wrong desires, wrong deeds, and wrong attitudes, children come under all sorts of negative influences that end up bringing serious problems into the home.

We see confirmation of all this in crime statistics. Back in 1950, adults committed serious crimes at a rate of 215 times the number of serious crimes committed by children who were 14 years of age or younger. During that entire year, 170 children were arrested for serious crimes. As a percentage, children committed only .0004 percent of all serious crimes.[6]

Between 1950 and 1960, homes all across America bought their first televisions. And as electronic media began to have its impact, we note that by 1960, serious adult crimes were committed at a rate of only 8 times the number of serious crimes by children. In just ten years, the ratio went from 215 to 1 to 8 to 1. By 1979, the ratio was 5.5 to 1. And that's just serious crimes. During that same time span, there was an 8300 percent increase in lesser offenses committed by children.[7] We hear all the time now about children who are arrested for serious crimes at younger and younger ages—crimes such as bank holdups, rape, and even first-degree murder.

All this has happened because our children live in a society whose psychological and social contexts have diminished the differences between adults and children. As the adult world opens itself in every conceivable way to children, those who are young will inevitably emulate adults more and more—for both good and bad.

This holds true for adult immorality and addictions as well. Teen pregnancy has run rampant, and alcohol and drug use are widespread not just among teens but preteens as well. We read every now and then about girls as young as 12 or 13 years old who are giving birth to babies, and kids not even 10 years old who are using alcohol or drugs. It's all because we have children who are overexposed to influences that are inappropriate for them.

That gives us some idea of the challenges parents face when it comes to external cultural influences that can harm their children.

The Internal Pressure of the Fallen Human Nature

All that outside pressure upon our families is compounded even more by the internal pressures that come from within our children themselves. While our kids may start out in life with a certain amount of ignorance and naïveté concerning certain issues, they are not born innocent with regard to evil. Our children are born sinners, and the seed of every known sin is planted deep in the heart of every child.

The common perception is that if we as parents don't do our jobs, our children might mess up their lives. But the truth is that our children are *already* messed up from birth. The issue isn't that they might drift spiritually and wander morally as they get older. Rather, the drive to sin is already embedded in their nature as fallen human beings.

Children don't come into the world seeking God and righteousness. Rather, from birth they seek the fulfillment of their sinful desires. Given the opportunity, children will give expression to these desires. The natural bent of humans, from the time they are born, is to commit sin. As Romans 3:11-12 says, "There is none who seeks God...there is none who does good, there is not even one."

When we hear about mass murderers, pedophiles, rapists, and people who exhibit lifelong chronic criminal behavior, frequently the question is asked, "What did their parents do to them when they were children?" The assumption is that those who become hardened criminals were raised in an abusive environment. And while that might be true, the issue isn't so much what their parents *did* do, but what they *didn't* do.

> The natural bent of humans, from the time they are born, is to commit sin.

Those who turn to a life of crime do so because they are just following the natural course of their sinful nature. When parents don't discipline their children and punish them for wrongdoing, it opens the door for their children to give full expression to the depravity that already resides within. That's what can happen when there is a lack of proper parental instruction and influence, as well as a lack of the kind of spiritual guidance that would lead children to repent of sin and receive Christ as their Savior.

The Bible clearly dispels the notion that children are born innocent. For example, in Psalm 58:3-4 we read, "The wicked are estranged from the womb; those who speak lies go astray from birth. They have venom like the venom of a serpent." That is not speaking of a singular reprobate subclass of humanity whom the Bible designates unusually "wicked." It's describing the state of the entire race after Adam's fall. "The intent of man's heart is evil from his youth" (Genesis 8:21). "There is none righteous, not even one" (Romans 3:10). "For all have sinned and fall short of the glory of God" (verse 23). "Indeed, there is not a righteous man on earth who continually does good and who never sins" (Ecclesiastes 7:20). "If we say that we have no sin, we are deceiving ourselves and the truth is not in us" (1 John 1:8).

Even the most respectable and principled people are fallen and guilty and have the potential for all kinds of evil in their hearts. In Psalm 51:5, King David said, "I was brought forth in iniquity, and in sin my mother conceived me." David wasn't saying he was an illegitimate child; he was declaring that from the time of conception he was a sinner. It was a guilty man's confession that he was thoroughly and totally depraved. His very nature was bent toward sinning.

Simply stated, humans are wicked from the time they come out of the womb. They are liars from birth. And their words and actions are like the poisonous venom in a serpent's fangs.

Proverbs 22:15 states, "Foolishness is bound up in the heart of a child; the rod of discipline will remove it far from him." In other words, foolishness is already a part of our children's nature. It's bound up in their hearts. As parents, our job is to instruct, admonish, and discipline them in such a way that they learn to do what is right and reject the internal, fleshly impulse to do wrong.[8]

Understanding the total depravity of your children is fundamental to helping them get onto the path of right living. While it's possible to bring your children under some level of control by teaching them moral virtues and punishing them for wrong behavior, ultimately what you want to do is see them pass from darkness to light. You want to see their hearts transformed by Christ so that instead of loving sin they love righteousness. Instead of wanting to give in to their evil desires, they want to give expression to what honors God.

That's why many of the practical issues of raising children—such as what kind of schedule you put them on for naps and bedtime—are really of little consequence. No scheduling method, coaching technique, or developmental program is going to rid your children of the sin in their hearts. In everything you do as a parent, your focus should be to lead your children to the transforming grace of Jesus Christ. God has not given us little angels to be handled carefully lest they get corrupted. They're already sinners who need to be led to salvation and faith in Christ.

Even the secular world, to some extent, realizes that children are prone to choose wrong over right. And what is the response of psychologists, child-care specialists, educators, and other secular pundits? They tell us the problem is our children don't have enough self-esteem. Misbehaving kids are simply revealing that they don't have enough self-love or a strong enough sense of self-worth. They need to see themselves as good, noble, wonderful people. They need to think more highly of themselves. So when children do wrong, we shouldn't tell them they are guilty or punish them. Instead, we should give them encouragement; we ought to say, "You need to love and accept yourself the way you are."

But that approach only pours gasoline on the fire, because young people already have a bent toward sin—including a tendency to sinful self-love. Stoking their fallen egos only encourages them to give in to their own destructive tendencies and do whatever feels good to them. Instead of encouraging children toward growth and improvement, we are permitting them to exercise selfishness and have their own way no matter what.

So prevalent is the mantra of self-esteemism today that we find it embedded all throughout popular culture. It is the dominant message in many self-improvement books, popular TV shows, contemporary songs, motivational lectures, educational programs, and more. It's why some children's sports leagues are set up so there are no losers (or winners, for that matter). It's why many schools use grading systems that ensure no one will fail. In fact, one self-esteem technique some schools use is called "inventive spelling." When a child spells a word wrong, he is not corrected for fear it will stifle his ability to express himself in writing. (I admit I practiced inventive spelling when I was in elementary school, but back then, none of my teachers seemed to appreciate the creative genius behind what I was doing.)

All the self-esteem movement has done is tell people it's okay to feel good about however they express themselves. That kind of message only encourages out-of-control behavior. Kids are told they can do whatever they want and feel okay about it. This has given us a generation of people who are driven toward the personal fulfillment of whatever self-ish desires they have in their hearts. But the Bible has nothing positive to say about self-esteem, self-love, or any other variety of self-centeredness. Instead, Scripture teaches us to confess our sins (1 John 1:9); to deny ourselves (Luke 9:23); to regard others as more important than ourselves (Philippians 2:3); and to cultivate the same kind of humility and self-sacrifice Christ exemplified (verses 5-8).

When it comes to raising children, then, parents are faced with two enormous pressures—the external pressure that a corrupt world places upon their kids, and the internal pressure of a corrupt nature within their kids' hearts. Fail to deal with these pressures, and the results will be tragic.

With that as a backdrop—knowing that the doctrine of total depravity is a fundamental tenet of Pauline theology, and knowing how thoroughly the apostle despised worldly values—we can appreciate the profound simplicity of this single-sentence nugget of advice for fathers in Ephesians 6:4: "Fathers, do not provoke your children to anger, but bring them up in the discipline and instruction of the Lord."

God's Perfect Pattern for Raising Children

Ephesians 6:4 tells us exactly what we need to know if our desire is to lead our children to Christ and build them up toward spiritual maturity. It's a dual imperative—a negative command paired with a positive one. When we make that twin directive our top priority, we will give our children the help they need to respond properly to both the external and internal pressures they face in their lives. In short, there is no greater favor we can do for our kids than to let this simple verse govern all our parenting.

A Responsibility for Both Parents

At first glance it might appear this verse speaks only to fathers, but the word translated "fathers" is the Greek term *pateres*, which can refer to fathers in particular but is often used to speak of both parents. So this principle applies equally to both the mother and the father. Yet in light of the fact that you as a father are vested with the role of leadership in the home, ultimately the manner in which you and your wife agree to raise your children starts with you. You are also the one who will answer to God for leadership in your family. While your job commitments may mean that your wife does more of the day-to-day nurture and admonition of your children, by virtue of your role as leader of the home, you bear the responsibility of making decisions about how you and your wife discipline and instruct your children. And you need to affirm and actively reinforce all that your wife does in carrying out those decisions. You cannot be passive in the parenting process.

A Responsibility to Reach Your Children for Christ

That you are to teach your children "in the discipline and instruction of the Lord" means first and foremost that you must be an evangelist in your home. Your kids need to be taught that they are sinners who are alienated from God, and that they will feel impulses that are wrong and dishonoring to God. They also need to be shown clearly the consequences of their sin, which includes the forfeiture of blessing, difficulty in life, eventual death, and eternity in hell separated from God. Children need to know all that.

Some parents think it's enough to tell their children that Jesus wants to be their friend. But you cannot tell your kids about God's grace and forgiveness unless they know about His law and judgment. They won't understand their need for salvation until they realize their sin separates them from God. They need to be aware they have violated God's law and they have no capacity within themselves to keep that law and please God. They need to realize that just trying to keep the law externally won't work because it's their heart that needs to be transformed, not just their outer behavior.

Your children need to know that because they are sinners, they are destined for eternal punishment unless they put their trust in Jesus Christ and their sins are forgiven. Only then can they live with the hope of a future in heaven. So as a parent, your first task is to pursue vigorously the eternal salvation of your children.

You may be wondering, "What if my kids are little? Might the gospel be too hard for them to understand? Should I somehow abbreviate the gospel message when I share it with them?"

There's no biblical reason to alter the good news for little children. What's important is that you use terminology they can grasp. You want to be clear and patient in communicating the message. Don't drown your kids in a sea of verbiage or crush them under the weight of complex theological arguments.

When Scripture talks about evangelizing your children, the emphasis is placed on being thorough and persistent. For example, Deuteronomy 6:6-7 says this:

These words, which I am commanding you today,
shall be on your heart. You shall teach them diligently to your sons and shall talk of them when you
sit in your house and when you walk by the way and
when you lie down and when you rise up.

You must constantly teach your children the truth about
God, judgment, grace, forgiveness, and salvation. This is to
be done when you sit down, as you are walking, when you lie
down, and when you get up. In other words, there is no time
when teaching your children biblical truth is inappropriate.
You don't need to overwhelm them with complex discussions,
but you don't want to be too simplistic, either. You don't want
to shortchange your children's understanding of the gospel
and what it means to be saved from their sins.

People often ask me, "At what age should I do this with my
children?" Clearly, children are not able to come to salvation
until they're old enough to understand the gospel message and
embrace it with genuine faith. But start as soon as they are
mature enough to understand sin, repentance, faith, and punishment. They need to be old
enough to understand the seri-
ousness of their sin and the
nature of God's holy standard.
The age for this will vary from
child to child. As you start with
the basic concepts and keep
teaching your children, God will do His work. Eventually
your kids will reach the point of clear comprehension. Along
the way, you will see encouraging responses and childlike

> As you start with the
> basic concepts and keep
> teaching your children,
> God will do His work.

expressions of trust. Affirm and encourage every step toward mature faith. But don't make the mistake of thinking your children's eternal destiny is settled if someone persuades them to ask Jesus into their hearts, raise a hand after a Bible lesson, or otherwise show an interest in having Jesus as a friend. You're looking for that moment when your children truly have a clear picture of where they stand with God—when they feel the weight of their guilt, see the beauty of Christ's righteousness, and with repentant faith embrace Him as their own Lord and Savior.

As a matter of fact, teaching your kids to invite Jesus into their hearts is far from what Paul has in mind when he commands fathers to raise their children "in the discipline and instruction of the Lord." He's clearly describing a steady process of guidance and mentoring—not a single rote prayer recited like a magic formula. Sinners—including children—are saved only by grace through *faith*. Works—including prayers—save no one. It's quite true that saving faith is childlike in the sense that it involves humble, unquestioning trust (Matthew 18:3-4). But faith cannot exist at all where the truth of the gospel is unknown (Romans 10:14). Authentic faith comes with spiritual understanding (1 John 5:20). Don't assume your child's earliest signs of interest in Jesus signify full-grown saving faith. I've known countless people who "invited Jesus into their hearts" as toddlers only to fall away from Christ before faith could come to full fruition. Again, both Ephesians 6:4 and Deuteronomy 6:7 employ expressions that underscore the need for persistence, faithfulness, and diligence in the nurture and admonition of our children. Don't abandon the task, thinking you have fulfilled your duty, just because your children seem friendly toward Jesus at a very young age.

In addition, don't soften the parts of the gospel message that sound unpleasant. Let your kids know about hell and judgment, the reason Christ died on the cross, and the need for an atonement for our sins. Explain it in language they can understand. Don't tone down the need for a commitment to Christ or complete surrender to His Lordship.

Now specifically, what do you tell them? What sort of information do your children need to know? Let me give you a basic outline to follow:

Teach Your Children About God's Holiness

Teach your children that God is a holy God. He is without sin, never does anything wrong, and cannot look upon iniquity. You can share the following Scripture passages with them:

> *Leviticus 11:44*—"I am the LORD your God. Consecrate yourselves therefore, and be holy, for I am holy."
> *1 Samuel 2:2*—"There is no one holy like the LORD."
> *1 Samuel 6:20*—"Who is able to stand before the LORD, this holy God?"
> *Matthew 5:48*—"You are to be perfect, as your heavenly Father is perfect."
> *1 Peter 1:15-16*—"Be holy yourselves also in all your behavior; because it is written, 'You shall be holy, for I am holy.'"
> *Hebrews 12:14*—"Without holiness no one will see the Lord" (NIV).

Explain to your children that God is absolutely holy and has set an absolutely holy standard for anyone to stand in His presence. If you ask them whether they are perfect like God, they will know they're not.

Because God is holy, He hates sin and will judge sinners, who cannot come into His presence.

> *Habakkuk 1:13*—"Your eyes are too pure to approve evil, and You can not look on wickedness with favor."
> *Psalm 1:5*—"The wicked will not stand in the judgment, nor sinners in the assembly of the righteous."

Teach Your Children About Their Sin

Help your children to understand they have fallen short of God's perfect standard. The only way they can receive God's forgiveness is to turn away from their sin. Explain that the gospel is a message of forgiveness to otherwise doomed people who are destined to eternal punishment in hell.

So that your children can gain an understanding of what sin is, talk with them about specific sins, bad attitudes, lies, and their failure to obey God or their parents. Explain that the reason they sin is that sin dwells in their heart. They need to understand that no matter how good they try to be, they will still fall short of God's perfect standard. That's because they are sinners by nature, and only through faith in Christ can their heart be cleansed.

Make it clear that everyone in the world is in the same situation so you don't give the impression they're alone in this. Let them know there was a time you too needed to recognize your need for Christ to forgive your sins. In fact, share with them how you came to realize your need for a Savior, and how you became a Christian.

Explain that Christ came to earth specifically to call sinners to Himself. Jesus said, "I did not come to call the righteous, but sinners" (Mark 2:17). He came because there is nothing people can do to earn their salvation. Good works aren't enough. According to Romans 3:20, "By the works of the Law no flesh will be justified in His sight." Galatians 2:16 says, "A man is not justified by the works of the Law but through faith in Christ Jesus." As sinners, we are completely helpless before God.

Teach Your Children What Christ Did for Them

Tell your children the story of Jesus. Explain that He is God Himself and came to earth in human flesh and lived among us (John 1:1,14). "God so loved the world, that He gave His only begotten Son, that whoever believes in Him shall not perish, but have eternal life" (John 3:16).

Make sure your kids understand who Jesus is:

> *Acts 10:36*—"He is Lord of all."
> *Philippians 2:10-11*—"At the name of Jesus every knee will bow, of those who are in heaven and on earth and under the earth, and…every tongue will confess that Jesus Christ is Lord."
> *Revelation 17:14*—"He is Lord of lords and King of kings."

Philippians 2:5-7 explains how "Christ Jesus, who, although He existed in the form of God, did not regard equality with God a thing to be grasped, but emptied Himself, taking the form of a bond-servant, and being made in the likeness of men." He came into the world and took on human form, and was "tempted in all things as we are, yet without sin" (Hebrews 4:15). He lived a pure and sinless life. First Peter 2:22

says He "committed no sin, nor was any deceit found in His mouth." And 1 John 3:5 says, "In Him there is no sin."

Tell your children that the eternal God, who is Lord of all, became man and lived an absolutely sinless life. He then died on the cross to become a sacrifice for our sins. Second Corinthians 5:21 says that God the Father "made Him [Jesus] who knew no sin to be sin on our behalf, so that we might become the righteousness of God in Him." Jesus became the sacrifice for us and took God's punishment for our sins. That's why Jesus died on the cross—to bear all our sins and provide a way for us to be reconciled to God.

Three days after His crucifixion, Jesus was raised from the dead—"He who was delivered over because of our transgressions...was raised because of our justification" (Romans 4:25). Jesus' death satisfied the justice of God, and He rose from the grave. In all this Jesus conquered sin, death, and Satan. With Jesus' help, we can have forgiveness of our sins and go to heaven.

Teach Your Children What God Asks Them to Do in Response

So how are your children to respond to the gospel message? God calls them to repent and trust Jesus as Lord and Savior. Acts 16:31 says, "Believe in the Lord Jesus, and you will be saved." Urge your children to put their trust in Christ and to seek Him while they can, before it's too late.

The Greatest Privilege as Parents

Even very young children can understand these truths if you explain them simply and clearly. Sharing the gospel with them is no different from sharing it with an adult. And key to it all is sharing this in a loving home environment. Keep sharing the gospel with them and, as opportunity allows, share with them about your own faith. Keep in mind that the hearts of children are more tender, more eager, more responsive because they're not filled with years of accumulated selfishness, worldliness, and cultivated lusts.

What a tremendous privilege it is to lead your kids to Christ! That's a foundational step in fulfilling the command given to parents in Ephesians 6:4: "Fathers, do not provoke your children to anger, but bring them up in the discipline and instruction of the Lord." May you seek to carry out this responsibility in a loving, tender, and patient manner so that you might be among those who raise up a new generation that seeks to love the Lord and bring glory to Him.

The essence of parental love is recognizing that we are the dispensers of God's grace into our children's lives. They learn to identify and reverence God's character through the way we treat them both in moments of profound pride and in times of intense disappointment.[9]

BRYAN CHAPELL

Chapter 3

Raising Your Children in the Lord, Part 2

As we continue our look at Ephesians 6:4 to learn about God's perfect pattern for raising our children, it's vital that we remember the bigger context of the book of Ephesians. This is a book that calls us, as Christians, to live differently—we are not to live as the world lives. We are to walk in God's light and not the world's darkness. We are to live according to God's wisdom and not the world's foolishness. We are to walk in the Spirit and not the flesh. We are to live distinctly because we are children of God who possess the Spirit of God and live according to the Word of God.

Right from the beginning of Ephesians, we're told that God "chose us in Him before the foundation of the world, that we would be holy and blameless before Him" (1:4). We are told God "works all things...to the praise of His glory"—that the purpose of His bringing us to salvation is to bring Him glory (1:11-14). He saved us so that we might carry out "good works, which God prepared beforehand so that we would walk in them" (2:10). For these reasons, we are exhorted "to walk in a manner worthy of the calling with which you have been called" (4:1). We are to "lay aside the old self…and put on the new self, which [is] in the likeness of God" (4:22-24). We are to be "imitators of God" (5:1) who "walk as children of Light" (verse 8).

It is after all these exhortations to holy living that we come to God's perfect pattern for marriage and the family in Ephesians 5:22–6:4. So the lifestyle to which God has called us as Christians should influence every relationship in the family. When it comes to living out our roles as spouses and parents, we shouldn't act the way unbelievers do. Nor should we succumb to the pressures of how the world tells us we ought to conduct our family life. Our standard for the family is completely different—it's found in the Bible, and it comes from God Himself.

So rather than listen to flawed human wisdom and contemporary society's diagnoses, we are to follow God's prescription. It is summed up magnificently for us in this simple statement in Ephesians 6:4: "Fathers, do not provoke your children to anger, but bring them up in the discipline and instruction of the Lord." This is not the message of conventional wisdom, political correctness, or secular psychology. It's what God Himself says.

> Our standard for the family is completely different—it's found in the Bible, and it comes from God Himself.

It only makes sense that we should follow God's Word when it comes to raising our children because He is the one who gave them to us. Psalm 127:3 tells us, "Behold, children are a gift of the LORD." They are gifts from God, and they are given to be a blessing to us.

But how often do children become a source of heartache because God's pattern for parenting is not properly followed? God has given us the directive in Ephesians 6:4 so that we might bring our children to the place where they will honor Him. That is why it's so vital that you build all your parenting efforts around this simple admonishment to "not provoke your children to anger, but bring them up in the discipline and instruction of the Lord."

The Priorities of a Christian Parent

Within Ephesians 6:4 we find both a negative instruction and a positive one. We'll start with the negative, which is stated first: "Fathers, do not provoke your children to anger."

Do Not Provoke Your Children to Anger

The instruction "do not provoke your children to anger" was a revolutionary concept in the pagan culture to which the apostle Paul was writing. At the time, Roman law gave fathers absolute power over their families—it was called *patria potestas* (Latin for "power of a father"). A father could rule with absolute authority and had no obligation to consider the welfare and desires of his wife and children. In fact, when a child was born, the father had say over whether to let the baby live or die by exposure. A father could do whatever he wanted to his children. He could punish them however he wanted, or even sell them into slavery or have them executed no matter what their age.

In addition, infanticide was a common practice in ancient

Rome and wasn't outlawed until AD 374. We learn from the Roman orator Seneca that weak and deformed children were drowned. Some historians say abandoned babies were sometimes picked up by people who would then nourish them and raise them to be slaves and prostitutes.

So Paul was writing to a world in which children were commonly abused and even murdered. As much as people would like to think we are a lot more cultured today, we're not—with the tragic legalization of abortion, we're not all that different from the ancient Romans. What's more, many parents today see children as an inconvenience. Some say if they had to do it all over again, they wouldn't have kids. And then there are children who live in foster homes not because their parents are dead, but because they're unwanted. One of the major contributors to teen suicide is that children feel rejected or even hated by their parents. So there is plenty of hostility toward children in our day as well.

It is against this backdrop of animosity toward children that the Bible commands, "Fathers, do not provoke your children to anger." In other words, don't exasperate them. Don't make unreasonable demands upon them. Don't do things that will drive them to anger, despair, or resentment. Paul's words about provoking a child suggest a repeated, ongoing pattern of behavior on the part of the parents that, over time, builds up and makes a child more and more frustrated and angry.

At this point I'd like to interject a couple of key cautionary thoughts. First, while Ephesians 6:4 applies equally to both parents, frequently it's the father who, by virtue of his leadership in the home, may end up provoking a child to anger, whether intentionally or not. Among the more common ways to provoke a child is through unrealistic rules in the home or excessive discipline. Because it is often the father who sets the rules or carries out discipline, it's easy for him to be the one who does the provoking, even if inadvertently. This calls for you as a father to be especially careful in your interactions with your children.

Second, you may be quick to say, "I would never intentionally provoke my child to anger." But it's easy to be guilty of this even when we have the best of intentions. For example, it can happen when we place too many restrictions on our children. One of the challenges of parenting is the frequent need to adjust our guidance and rules so that they are commensurate with our children's age and maturity.

How else do we unintentionally provoke our children? There are many ways, and I'm going to list ten of the more common ones here. As you go through the list, you may realize additional ways you need to be cautious in your parenting.

By Being Overprotective

If you want to exasperate your kids, restrict them and don't trust them. Don't allow them the opportunity to develop their independence. Keep them under stern control at all times. But if you want your children to be happy and enjoy life, give them room to express themselves, discover their world, and experience new adventures. Be willing to let go of them gradually as they mature.

By Showing Favoritism

Remember how, in the Old Testament, Isaac favored Esau over Jacob? And Isaac's wife, Rebekah, did the opposite—she favored Jacob over Esau. The sad results of this unfortunate favoritism are well-known. Jacob cheated Esau out of his inheritance, and this infuriated Esau. Jacob had to run away from home to protect himself from Esau's vengeance, and Rebekah never saw Jacob again.

Don't compare your children with one another. Don't say things like, "Why can't you be more like your brother?" Or, "Why isn't your room as clean as your sister's?" If one child has any reason to think that you love another child more, that will create deep feelings of hurt and rejection.

By Setting Unrealistic Achievement Goals

Some parents crush their children by putting them under too much pressure to excel in school, sports, music, or whatever it is they do. Often this pressure has little to do with the child and everything to do with the parents' pride or reputation.

Children get very frustrated when they feel there's just no way they can make their parents happy. No matter how hard they try, the parents just aren't satisfied. The bar is continually set higher, and there's no sensitivity to a child's abilities or skill levels. This can cause anger and bitterness.

Back when my sons were young and played in organized sports, I remember seeing fathers who would belittle their sons for their performance on the field. No matter how well the kids played, their dads were critical. This instilled fear and frustration in those children, who ended up finding it difficult to perform well in games.

Some years ago I met a very accomplished teenage girl who ended up killing herself because her mother was so critical of everything she did. She had been an outstanding student and was very involved at her school. But the pressure from her mother caused her to have a severe breakdown that required medical treatment in an institution. Upon returning home, the criticisms resumed, and the daughter eventually took her own life. Why? Before her final breakdown, she said to me, "No matter what I do, it never satisfies my mother."

Dads, we need to make sure we don't push our kids to the point of self-destructive anger.

By Allowing Them to Be Overindulgent

You can frustrate your children to anger by giving them everything they want, picking up after them all the time, and allowing them to shift all responsibility and accountability for their behavior onto others. You can overindulge them by letting them sin and get away with it, which will encourage them to do it repeatedly. But when it comes time for them to face the world on their own and people don't serve them or allow them to deflect responsibility for their misdeeds, they will lash out in anger.

By Discouragement

This can happen in two ways: (1) a lack of understanding on your part, and (2) a lack of rewards for your children. Both will destroy your children's motivation and incentive. That's why it's vital that you take the time to understand your kids. Take time to determine why they are acting a certain way, or what they're trying to accomplish. Give them a listening ear, and reward them graciously with love. Give them approval and honor when it's appropriate, and be patient with them. Don't raise the bar of your expectations unrealistically high, and don't respond to them in ways that will cause them to feel defeated or discouraged.

By Failing to Make Sacrifices for Them

Another way to provoke your children to anger is by making them feel like they are an intrusion into your life. Whether overtly or subtly, you communicate to them that they are a bother because they get in the way of what you want to do or where you want to go. You look forward to dropping them off at someone else's house or sending them out on some activity so you are free to do your own thing. You want to have your own fun and pleasure, and the kids will just have to fend for themselves. You tell them to prepare their own meals and not to interrupt you because what you're doing is more important. When you are uncaring and unavailable in these ways, your children will come to resent you.

By Failing to Allow Them to Grow Up

Children aren't perfect. They've got a lot to learn, and they're going to make mistakes along the way. So they knock something over at the table—laugh it off. They are still developing their dexterity and coordination. When you ask your kids to do something and they don't do it quite right, don't jump all over them for it. Come alongside them, commend them for giving it a try, and teach them how to do it better next time. Expect progress, not perfection.

By Neglect

One well-known biblical illustration of parental neglect is the relationship between King David and his son Absalom. Evidently David was so busy that he spent no time with his son, for Absalom grew up with contempt for his father and other members of the family. He rebelled against David's authority as king and set up an elaborate plot to dethrone him. The sordid details of his deeds are chronicled for us in 2 Samuel chapters 13–18. In the end, Absalom was slain in battle.

David's neglect was certainly not a case of willful indifference. He clearly had a profound love for Absalom. We're told in 2 Samuel 18:33 that David wept greatly over his son's death. The loss of his son was one of David's greatest heartaches. As a father, you need to make sure your children are constantly aware of your love for them. It's not enough just to know, within your own mind and heart, that you love them. Instead, you need to clearly verbalize your love and demonstrate it through time spent with them and showing an interest in their lives.

When my sons Matt and Mark were growing up, I had a special agreement with them. I made a commitment to go to their games. And they, in turn, came to church to hear my sermons. We were involved in each other's worlds, and as a result we were able to cultivate strong and close father-son relationships that endure to this day.

In the previous chapter, I mentioned that usually when we look at hardened criminals, our first thought is, *What did their parents do to make them turn out that way?* But, as we noted, the problem isn't necessarily what the parents *did*, but what they *didn't* do. When children are neglected and left undisciplined, adults like Absalom are the result.

By Abusive Words

Verbal abuse can have a profound impact on children. With mere words, it's very easy for a parent to cut a little child's heart to shreds. This can include words spoken in anger, sarcasm, or ridicule. Some parents say things to their children they would never say to anyone else. And the kids are usually unable to defend themselves because they just don't know how to respond. Their feelings are hurt and crushed, and they come away from verbal abuse feeling rejected. Over time, such treatment will generate bitterness and provoke a child to rebellion.

By Physical Abuse

Some parents are overzealous when it comes to punishing their children and actually beat them. They go beyond reasonable, appropriate measures to discipline their kids and end up harming them. This is the worst form of bullying and brutality, because parents should be the ones most devoted to the child's love and protection. When instead they injure and otherwise abuse their own children, the damage is immeasurable. As if physical injury to the child were not bad enough, such abuse does lasting harm to the child's spirit. Throwing your weight around and taking advantage of what is an obvious physical mismatch will fill a child with fear. A child who is physically abused is sure to grow up with a vengeful spirit toward his parents and will unleash a similar brutality upon others around him when he grows older.

In Hebrews 12:5-7, we read that God disciplines His children in love. When our heavenly Father corrects us, love is always His preeminent attitude. The chastisement may be painful, but we know it's just and with good reason. When you discipline your children, make sure you don't do so when you're angry or feeling vengeful. Make sure you assess the situation first to determine an appropriate response. Ask the Lord for a calm mind and loving heart, and strive for your rebuke to emanate from a genuine compassion and concern for your child's well-being.

Those are just ten of the ways it's possible for parents to provoke a child to anger—there are plenty more. Regardless of how it is done, ultimately, provoking a child will exasperate him and drive him away. It will build a destructive attitude of resentment in his heart and, in the long run, will destroy your family.

Having addressed the first half of God's pattern for parenting as found in Ephesians 6:4, let's look at the second half, or the positive component:

Bring Up Your Children in the Discipline and Instruction of the Lord

In the previous chapter we learned about the tremendous external and internal pressures our children face as they're growing up. They are surrounded by the corrupting influences of the world, and they struggle with the sinful desires within their hearts. These external and internal pressures are constant, and they will make our parenting a challenge. In light of this, God gives us the following admonishment so that we might raise our children in the right way: "Bring them up in the discipline and instruction of the Lord" (Ephesians 6:4). If we are to have any hope of raising our children so that they live righteous lives and bring honor to God, it's absolutely essential that we follow this guideline.

The phrase "bring them up" alludes to the fact our kids cannot grow up right on their own. Our proactive involvement in leading, guiding, and nurturing them is essential.

Proverbs 29:15 says, "A child left to himself brings shame to his mother" (NKJV). So once again, it is not so much what parents *do* to their children that shapes them; it's also what they *don't* do. A lack of discipline and instruction will leave a child adrift and vulnerable to the world's negative influences. You are called to have a deliberate and ongoing focus on molding your children's lives.

We find Paul's use of the terms "discipline" and "instruction" helpful as well. The Greek word translated "discipline" is *nouthesia*, which speaks of rebuke or warning. This conveys the idea of gentle, loving parental admonishment. And the word translated "instruction" is *paideia*, which the King James Version renders as "nurture." When

> You are called to have a deliberate and ongoing focus on molding your children's lives.

you admonish and nurture your children, you will fulfill the responsibility described for you in Ephesians 6:4.

So what does this look like in everyday parenting? How do we bring up our children "in the discipline and instruction of the Lord"?

Watching Over Your Child's Heart

Proverbs 4:23 cuts right to the key issue in all of our parenting—we are to "watch over [the] heart with all diligence, for from it flow the springs of life." Because all matters of life proceed from the heart, we are to pay careful attention to our children's hearts.

In Mark 7:21-23, Jesus said, "For from within, out of the heart of men, proceed the evil thoughts, fornications, thefts, murders, adulteries, deeds of coveting and wickedness, as well as deceit, sensuality, envy, slander, pride and foolishness. All these evil things proceed from within and defile the man."

Our Lord commented further on this in Luke 6:45: "The good man out of the good treasure of his heart brings forth what is good; and the evil man out of the evil treasure brings forth what is evil; for his mouth speaks from that which fills his heart."

When it comes to raising our children, we need to recognize they have a heart problem. Every time they do wrong, it's a manifestation of what's in the heart. It's never enough simply to deal with their behavior and get them to look good on the outside. We need to address the condition of their hearts. If all we do is focus on their behavior, then the sin and rebellion that resides in their hearts will eventually surface and express itself.

That's why your children need to understand that they have a sinful heart. If they wonder where their evil words, thoughts, and deeds come from, tell them it's from the corruption within their heart. And that heart has to be changed, which can only happen through salvation in Christ.

Tedd Tripp, in his book *Shepherding a Child's Heart*, says that the world's smallest battlefield is the child's heart, and the conquering of it calls for all-out hand-to-hand combat.[10] Your child's heart is a battlefield where sin and righteousness are in conflict. That is why it's never enough to deal with surface issues such as your child's lack of maturity, understanding, and experience. A child will never outgrow his depravity. His sin nature will persist in his heart until it's dealt with.

As you lead your children, any objective that falls short of dealing with the heart is nothing more than behavior modification. After all, non-Christian children can be taught to conform to a morally acceptable standard. And while it is important to teach children to obey, we cannot confuse that with the main goal, which is the salvation of our children and raising them up in the Lord.

This requires training your children to understand temptation and the need to resist it. Help them to realize that all wrong attitudes and behaviors come from the heart. When you punish your children for their external offenses, be sure you help them see that the root issue is their heart. Let them know they have offended not just you, but God as well. This will make it clear that they are accountable not only to you, but more importantly to God. Above all, teach them that God desires reconciliation with them through Jesus Christ (2 Corinthians 5:19).

All of this requires constant vigilance on your part as a father. As Deuteronomy 6:7 says, you're to "teach [God's words] diligently to your sons and shall talk of them when you sit in your house and when you walk by the way and when you lie down and when you rise up." In 2 Timothy 3:16, we see that "all Scripture is…profitable for teaching, for reproof, for correction, for training in righteousness." Bring God's Word into your everyday interactions with your children. And along the way, exercise discipline when necessary—loving and consistent rebuke that teaches your kids there is a consequence for their sins.

Pointing Your Child to God

Let's look more closely at Deuteronomy 6, where we find some practical specifics about how we are to instruct our children. You'll find some excellent guidelines here for helping cultivate your children's awareness and understanding of God.

Teach Your Children to Acknowledge God

Verse 4 begins, "Hear, O Israel! The LORD is our God, the LORD is one!" This is a call to the people of Israel to recognize God and that He alone is Lord. As such, He is totally sovereign. You want to teach your child about God and explain that He rules over everything. He alone is the supreme authority over all.

Teach Your Children to Love God

Verse 5 continues, "You shall love the LORD your God with all your heart and with all your soul and with all your might." It is essential that you instruct your children to love God. When they do, it will have an effect on their behavior. They will realize that to love God is to live in a way that pleases Him. This will make your children more reluctant to engage in sinful behavior.

Teach Your Children to Obey God

Verses 6-7 flow out of what we read in verse 5: "These words, which I am commanding you today, shall be on your heart. You shall teach them diligently to your sons." While you are to teach your children to obey the Lord, you want to instill in them a desire to obey out of love for God. When they love God, they will want to obey Him.

Teach Your Children to Follow Your Example

Verses 7-8 continue: "You shall teach them diligently to your sons and shall talk of them when you sit in your house and when you walk by the way and when you lie down and when you rise up." At all times, make God's Word a part of your speech, your attitudes, and your actions. Share the principles found in the Bible and live them out. Let your kids see that your life is dominated by God's truth. All of life is a classroom; everything that happens is an opportunity to point your children to the Scriptures.

Jesus was a master of using illustrations from everyday life to teach spiritual truth. He spoke of water, fig trees, mustard seeds, birds, bread, pearls, wheat, tares, vineyards, fishing nets, light, darkness, and so on to help people gain a clearer understanding of divine truth. When we do the same for our children, we sensitize them to see God's hand and hear His voice in the world around them. Everything in life can be used to help draw our children's attention to God.

Teach Your Children Through Ongoing Repetition

Note that the activity of teaching God's Word to your children should never cease. Deuteronomy 6:7 says to teach "when you sit in your house," "when you walk by the way," "when you lie down," "when you rise up." This speaks of ongoing, unceasing instruction that takes place day in and day out. In verses 8-9, God's people are told to take His Word and put it "on your hand...on your forehead...on the doorposts of your house." Later in Jewish history, these commands were taken literally and the people placed Scripture passages inside little boxes on their hands, foreheads, and doorposts. But God's point was that they were to continually meditate upon and be directed by His law.

Teach Your Children to Be Wary So They Don't Forget

The admonishments in Deuteronomy 6:4-9 then conclude with this warning:

> Then it shall come about when the LORD your God brings you into the land which He swore to your fathers, Abraham, Isaac and Jacob, to give you, great and splendid cities which you did not build, and houses full of all good things which you did not fill, and hewn cisterns which you did not dig, vineyards and olive trees which you did not plant, and you eat and are satisfied, then watch yourself, that you do not forget the LORD who brought you from the land of Egypt, out of the house of slavery (verses 10-12).

God tells Israel, "After you enter this land filled with good things, make sure you don't become distracted and forget Me." Likewise, as your children go out into the world and see all that there is to touch, explore, and experience, warn them so they don't become captivated by the things of the world and forget God. Continually point them to God, and alert them to the many things that can lure their attention away from Him.

This, in a practical way, is what it means to bring up your children "in the discipline and instruction of the Lord" (Ephesians 6:4). It involves getting them to acknowledge God and His sovereign rule over everything. It means exhorting your children to love God with all their heart, soul, and might. It means teaching them to obey God and follow your example. Do all this continually, using the classroom of life to help make biblical truth more memorable for them. And warn them so that the things of the world don't pull them away from following God.

The Need for a Changed Heart

Susannah Wesley had 17 children, including John and Charles, who went on to have widely influential ministries as evangelists and writers of books and hymns. She wrote:

> The parent who studies to subdue self-will in his child works together with God in the saving of a soul. The parent who indulges self-will does the devil's work, makes religion impractical, salvation unattainable, and does all that is in him to drown his child, soul and body forever.

Don't indulge your children when it comes to their self-will. Teach them that they are called to obey God, yet cannot do so without His grace at work in their hearts. Show them their sin, and explain that only God can change their hearts through faith in Jesus Christ. At every opportunity, encourage your children toward a personal relationship with the Lord.

At all times, your goal is not merely to modify your children's behavior, but to lead them to Christ so that God can change their hearts. From there onward you can bring up your children in the discipline and instruction of the Lord.

One father, looking at the parenting process in retrospect, said this: "If I were starting my family again, I would love my wife more in front of my children. I would laugh with my children more at our mistakes and our joys. I would listen to my children more, even to the littlest one. I would be more honest about my weaknesses and not pretend perfection. I would pray differently for my family. Rather than focusing on them, I'd focus on me. I would do more things with my children. I would do more encouraging. I would bestow more praise. I would pay more attention to little things. I would speak about God more intimately. Out of every ordinary thing of every ordinary day I would point them to God."

Did you notice this father didn't focus so much on his children's behavior? Instead, he emphasized being the right kind of example to his kids and leading them to God. He came to realize that the primary issue in parenting is the heart. That's what Scripture tells us.

Because only God can change the heart, the pattern given to us in Ephesians 6:4 makes perfect sense. That's the path we're to take as parents. It's given by God Himself, who possesses all wisdom and knows exactly how we as humans are wired because He created us. He knows what our kids need most.

When you as a father take His words to heart, you will have everything you need to raise children who are a joy and a blessing.

A true Christian must be no slave to fashion, if he would train his child for heaven. He must not be content to do things merely because they are the custom of the world;— to teach them and instruct them in certain ways, merely because it is usual;—to allow them to read books of a questionable sort, merely because everybody else reads them;—to let them form habits of a doubtful tendency, merely because they are the habits of the day. He must train with an eye to his children's souls. He must not be ashamed to hear his training called singular and strange. What if it is? The time is short—the fashion of this world passeth away. He that has trained his children for heaven, rather than for earth,—for God rather than for man,— he is the parent that will be called wise at the last.[11]

J.C. RYLE

Chapter 4

Leading Your Children to Grow in Wisdom

U p to this point, we have considered two Scripture passages that give us foundational guidelines for raising kids in the nurture and admonition of the Lord. The beauty of these passages is they are short and concise. In an economy of words, they cut right to the heart of a parent's most important priorities. To review:

> *Ephesians 6:4*—"Fathers, do not provoke your children to anger, but bring them up in the discipline and instruction of the Lord."

> *Deuteronomy 6:7*—"You shall teach [God's words] diligently to your sons and shall talk of them when you sit in your house and when you walk by the way and when you lie down and when you rise up."

Those passages provide for us the keys to successful Christian parenting. Anything else we find in Scripture about parenting will, in some way or other, tie back to these core principles. And that's what we're going to look at in the second half of this book—a variety of practical biblical guidelines that will help you as a father provide the kind of leadership that inspires a child to love and obey God.

A Manual for Parents

One place we can find a tremendous wealth of parental guidance is the book of Proverbs. There, we find a large collection of wise sayings and illustrations penned by King Solomon, all of which teach the fundamental realities of life. These are the basic principles of spiritual living. They are simple and direct—we could say they are full of wisdom in content, yet concise in form. They are pithy statements for the purpose of passing along instruction, and what makes them particularly useful is that they are easy to remember.

As we read through Proverbs we find that many of these wisdom sayings are instructions from parents to their children. More specifically, a large number of them are exhortations from a father to his son. For example:

> *Proverbs 1:8*—"Hear, my son, your father's instruction and do not forsake your mother's teaching."
> *Proverbs 2:1*—"My son, if you will receive my words..."
> *Proverbs 3:1*—"My son, do not forget my teaching."
> *Proverbs 4:1*—"Hear, O sons, the instruction of a father..."
> *Proverbs 4:10*—"Hear, my son, and accept my sayings..."
> *Proverbs 4:20*—"My son, give attention to my words..."
> *Proverbs 5:1*—"My son, give attention to my wisdom."
> *Proverbs 6:20*—"My son, observe the commandment of your father..."

Proverbs 7:1,3—"My son, keep my words and treasure my commandments within you...bind them on your fingers; write them on the tablet of your heart."

In the first several chapters of Proverbs, then, we see a caring father whose chief concern is to impart godly wisdom to his son. Here, we see the principles in Ephesians 6:4 and Deuteronomy 6:7 lived out. This father is passing on to his son the instruction of the Lord, and is making God's wisdom a practical and active part of his own life as well as his son's. If you as a father want to raise up godly sons and daughters who will, in turn, become part of a generation that will lead their families to godliness, you must actively teach them wisdom from God's Word. This is consistent with your main priority as a father.

When your kids look at you, do they see this as your main duty? Or do they simply perceive you as a breadwinner, or as the one who fixes the car, mows the lawn, takes out the trash? Based on your interactions with them day in and day out, would they guess that raising them up toward godliness is your first priority?

I am grateful to be able to say I could tell this was the priority for both my father and grandfather. They exemplified this in their lives to me. And I, in turn, made sure to do the same with my children—and now, my grandchildren. This is the key to raising successive generations of people who follow the Lord. This is the kind of leadership a father is called to. It's a high calling that comes from God Himself, one that ensures future righteous generations in the church.

The Focus on Wisdom

As we read Proverbs, we cannot help but notice that the word "wisdom" dominates all throughout the book. On occasion we'll see related words such as "instruction," "understanding," "discretion." But all of these are elements of wisdom. So there's a tremendous emphasis all through Proverbs on living wisely. And this wisdom isn't confined only to a person's thoughts, but extends to conduct as well. It is wisdom that leads a person to live righteously. As fathers, we are to teach our sons and daughters spiritual wisdom. To get our children to pursue wisdom is to encourage them in the noblest pursuit in life.

There are many other things you could teach your children. Visit the parenting section of your local bookseller and you'll find an abundance of advice, theories, instructions, methods, and techniques available for parents. But a lot of it is trivial—even much of what you'll find in books from respectable evangelical publishers. Typical parenting advice deals with life on a more superficial level—go places with your kids, follow their interests, play games with them. While doing such things can contribute toward building good family relationships, ultimately, they don't deal with

> To get our children to pursue wisdom is to encourage them in the noblest pursuit in life.

the spiritual condition of your children's hearts. If you never move beyond superficialities, how will you teach your kids what is truly important? And if they never understand the priorities of life, you won't be able to enjoy the incredible blessings that come with having kids who love and obey the Lord.

Teach your children divine wisdom from Scripture, and if they embrace the truth you give them, they'll become parents who teach their children divine wisdom. But teach them merely trivial things, and they will not only fail to learn life's most vital truths; they in turn will also teach their kids trivial things.

So the call of the whole book of Proverbs is a call to wisdom—not only for sons and daughters, but for parents as well. As a wise father, you want to teach and *show* your children that wisdom is of great value. As Proverbs 8:11 says, "Wisdom is better than jewels; and all desirable things cannot compare with her." The pursuit of wisdom is an enterprise that yields great benefits. Where will they learn that lesson, if not from their father?

As you lead in the home, then, a key priority for you is teaching your children wisdom. That's a big part of fulfilling the mandate in Ephesians 6:4 that you are to bring up your children "in the discipline and instruction of the Lord."

Ten Crucial Lessons Every Father Should Teach

For the rest of this chapter, we're going to look at Proverbs 1–10 and examine ten crucial lessons every Christian father should teach his kids. While these lessons primarily address sons, they can be made applicable to daughters as well. As your children learn how to apply these lessons to their lives, they will become a blessing to you, and they will be blessed by God.

1. Teach Your Children to Fear God

Proverbs 1:7 says, "The fear of the LORD is the beginning of knowledge." This truth is stated again in Proverbs 9:10: "The fear of the LORD is the beginning of wisdom." This tells us that the starting point for acquiring wisdom is a fear of God.

What exactly is meant by the term "fear"? There are two aspects to it. First, the positive aspect is that of reverential respect or awe for God. You instill this respect in your children by teaching them the attributes of God and letting them know that God is all-powerful, perfectly holy, all-knowing, and everywhere-present. He is immutable, which means His nature does not change. He is merciful, kind, loving, and gracious. He providentially orchestrates all of history for His ultimate good. He is sovereign. In short, He is not to be trifled with. The only proper response to a true understanding of God's nature is humble, awestruck, obedient worship—"with fear and trembling" (Philippians 2:12).

As you teach your children what God is like, they will come to know of His greatness. And they will come to fear Him in a positive, healthy way.

The second aspect of fearing the Lord is negative. It has to do with fearing God's displeasure—that is, His right to chastise and judge. Teach your children that God is holy and cannot tolerate sin. The fact God is both sovereign and holy gives Him the right to punish everyone's sins, including your children's.

One of the biggest favors you can do as a father is to teach your kids about the attributes of God. Once they understand who God is and what He is like, it will cultivate in them both a positive, reverential fear that worships Him and a negative, apprehensive fear that seeks to avoid offending Him. It will help your children to recognize that God is worthy of their respect and honor, and that He desires for them to live righteously.

It's not enough to tell your children God is great and worthy of our worship and obedience; you yourself must believe it, and show that you believe it in the way you live. Children are alert to whether their parents are consistent in their words and actions. Is that the case in your life? Do you worship faithfully on the Lord's day? Are you consistent in the practice of reading God's Word? Do your children look at you and see a true worshipper? The pattern of worship you have established for yourself is likely the same pattern your children will develop. What kind of legacy are you leaving?

Do you also live in a healthy fear of God's holy right to punish sin? Do you live in such a way that your children can tell you want to avoid bringing grief to God?

Proverbs 3:5-6 is instructive here: "Trust in the LORD with all your heart and do not lean on your own understanding. In all your ways acknowledge Him, and He will make your paths straight." This passage describes for us a worshipful heart—one that trusts God to the point of living in total submission to Him—"in all [our] ways," not merely when confronted with a crisis, in times of trouble, or on Sundays only. The point is that when your heart is truly and permanently anchored by trust in God and reverent love for Him, He will be your guide and guardian. He will "make your paths straight"—meaning He will make the way ahead clear and direct, seeing us through life's conflicts, confusion, and all kinds of spiritual road hazards.

In the original Hebrew text of the Old Testament, the

word translated "trust" means "to lie helplessly face down." It portrays a person who is fully bowed down before God and will do whatever God asks him to do. That's the kind of trust and humility we are called to. Are you teaching your children to trust God in everything—to fully lean on Him? When they exhibit that kind of trust, God will direct their paths. This is the kind of fear you want to instill in your children.

It's worth noting that when God is feared, sin is feared as well. A right fear of God fills the heart with a righteous fear and loathing for sin. Proverbs 8:13 says, "The fear of the LORD is to hate evil." When you love God, you're going to find yourself hesitant to do the things that displease Him.

2. Teach Your Children to Guard Their Minds

Proverbs 3:3-4 says, "Do not let kindness and truth leave you; bind them around your neck, write them on the tablet of your heart. So you will find favor and good repute in the sight of God and man." The Hebrew word translated "kindness," which is *hesed*, means "love, loyalty, faithfulness, fidelity, kindness." And the word translated "truth" is *'emet*, which means "truth, accuracy, reliability, dependability."

Proverbs 3:3-4 is urging us to take all these things and "bind them around your neck, write them on the tablet of your heart." Here, "heart" has reference to the mind, which is the seat of thought, emotion, and will. Ultimately, then, this passage is saying to teach your children to guard their minds.

Given the way today's culture is constantly assaulting the human mind—particularly in the area of electronic media—the job of guarding your children's minds is a formidable one. It's a tremendous responsibility that requires ongoing vigilance.

You're to be like the father who warned his son, "Watch over your heart with all diligence, for from it flow the springs of life" (Proverbs 4:23). In other words, tell your children to guard their minds, for that's the starting point of wrong thoughts and actions.

As Jesus said, "There is nothing outside the man which can defile him if it goes into him; but the things which proceed out of the man are what defile the man" (Mark 7:15). The issue is what comes out of the heart. That's why it's so important to program a child's mind with truth, virtue, faithfulness, honesty, integrity, loyalty, love, and other similar qualities. When you do this, you are guarding your children's minds.

Proverbs 1:9 says good instruction is like "a graceful wreath to your head and ornaments about your neck." When children wear truth in their hearts, it graces them. Proverbs 2:10-12 further states that "wisdom…will be pleasant to your soul; discretion will guard you, understanding will watch over you, to deliver you from the way of evil." A couple chapters later, in Proverbs 4:4, the father tells his son, "Let your heart hold fast my words; keep my commandments and live."

As a father, then, you are the guardian of your children's minds. Your duty before God is to protect their minds from all the worldly influences they are exposed to. At the same time, you are to help fill their minds with truth, kindness, and more by exposing them to God's Word. You are to tell them, "Guard your mind, for out of it comes your conduct."

3. Teach Your Children to Obey Their Parents

As we learned earlier, the first ten chapters of Proverbs contain multiple statements to the effect of "Hear, my son, your father's instruction." For example, in Proverbs 4:10-11 we read, "Hear, my son, and accept my sayings and the years of your life will be many. I have directed you in the way of wisdom; I have led you in upright paths." A little later in verses 20-21 we find this: "My son, give attention to my words; incline your ear to my sayings. Do not let them depart from your sight; keep them in the midst of your heart."

In all these instructions, the father is reinforcing "the first commandment with a promise," which is this: "Children, obey your parents in the Lord, for this is right" (Ephesians 6:1-2). The father in the book of Proverbs is saying, very simply, "Son, obey what I say."

This, of course, relates to the discipline aspect of the responsibilities laid out for parents in Ephesians 6:4. Note, for example, what the father says in Proverbs 3:11-12: "My son, do not reject the discipline of the LORD or loathe His reproof, for whom the LORD loves He reproves, even as a father corrects the son in whom he delights."

If you love your children, you will rebuke and discipline them. Why? So you can teach them to live righteously. Proverbs 22:15 says, "Foolishness is bound up in the heart of a child; the rod of discipline will remove it far from him." Proper discipline—which is done not in anger, but in love—will drive rebellion out of the heart of a child. In the same way that God disciplines those whom He loves, we are to rebuke our children in love. This is done to

> A child who is taught to obey will be a child who learns self-control and true wisdom.

help deliver a child from foolishness and spiritual death, and make him wise and a delight to his parents.

Ultimately, when your children learn to obey you, they will learn to obey societal authority and, more importantly, this is how they begin learning to obey God. They learn to submit to authority rather than break rules and engage in criminal behavior. A child who is taught to obey will be a child who learns self-control and true wisdom.

4. Teach Your Children to Select Their Companions Carefully

Here is a responsibility in which you as a father are to go on the offensive. You need to teach your children how to choose their friends. As the apostle Paul said, "Bad company corrupts good morals" (1 Corinthians 15:33). Your children cannot rise above their acquaintances. The friends your children associate with are going to determine the kind of people they will become. That's why it is so crucial to help your children learn how to select their companions, and not the other way around.

The father in the book of Proverbs was proactive about this. For example, in Proverbs 1:10 he said, "My son, if sinners entice you, do not consent." In other words, "Don't get sucked into the gang." He went on, "If they say, 'Come with us, let us lie in wait for blood, let us ambush the innocent without cause...we will find all kinds of precious wealth, we will fill our houses with spoil...My son, do not walk in the way with them'" (verses 11,13,15). The wicked will attempt to appeal to your children on the basis of excitement, adventure, and even the promise of ill gain. You are to train your children to resist such enticements.

It's tragic that there are people who are willing to inflict harm upon others or even take their lives just for a fleeting moment of pleasure. I remember reading about a young man in New York City who wouldn't take drugs with any of his so-called friends, so they set him on fire. Children and adolescents easily get pulled into foolish or wrong behavior through peer pressure. This pressure can be great, and the enticements can be strong. You must teach your children to select their companions so they don't end up being intimidated into the wrong kinds of alliances.

In Proverbs 2:11-13 the father tells his son, "Discretion will guard you, understanding will watch over you, to deliver you from the way of evil, from the man who speaks perverse things, from those who leave the paths of uprightness to walk in the ways of darkness." He warns his son not to hang around people who delight in doing evil. And a key way to prevent that from happening is to help his son gain discretion and understanding. These would protect and deliver him.

Equip your children with wisdom, and they will develop the discernment they need to choose their friends wisely.

5. Teach Your Children to Control Their Body

Any father who has any sense at all knows that young men are going to develop passions that can lead them into tragedy unless they learn how to control their bodily desires. How big of a potential problem is this? Big enough that it is *the* dominant theme throughout the first several chapters of Proverbs.

For example, in Proverbs 2:16-17 the father tells his son that wisdom will "deliver you from the strange woman, from the adulteress who flatters with her words; that leaves the companion of her youth and forgets the covenant of her God." The word "strange" here means "foreign." It refers to an immoral woman—a harlot. It was a common euphemism, adopted perhaps because the earliest prostitutes in Israel were foreigners who came into the land from the surrounding pagan nations. The language stuck, and the expression came to apply to any woman with loose morals—not just prostitutes, but also adulteresses, fornicators, and seductresses of all kinds. This passage goes on to describe a woman who has abandoned her marriage (forsaken "the companion of her youth") in order to instigate an affair with someone else. And she "forgets the covenant of her God," symbolized in the violation of her wedding vows. Such a woman is described with language that puts her on the level of a common prostitute.

The father then warns his son, "Her house sinks down to death and her tracks lead to the dead" (verse 18). Some think this may be a reference to the possibility one might get venereal disease, or suffer an act of punishment from God. Whatever the case, the destructive nature of adultery leads a person to devastating consequences, possibly including even death—a point reiterated in verse 19 ("None who go to her return again, nor do they reach the paths of life").

Some may think this too stern a warning, but it tells us there were men who were willing to succumb to sexual temptation even when they knew it could result in their death. Their lust for sex had outweighed their desire to live. That's how powerful sexual desires can be. Fathers are to teach their sons sexual self-control so they don't end up destroying their own lives or their families.

The father in Proverbs addresses the issue again in chapter 5:

> My son, give attention to my wisdom, incline your ear to my understanding; that you may observe discretion and your lips may reserve knowledge. For the lips of an adulteress drip honey and smoother than oil is her speech; but in the end she is bitter as wormwood, sharp as a two-edged sword. Her feet go down to death, her steps take hold of Sheol. She does not ponder the path of life; her ways are unstable, she does not know it (verses 1-6).

A woman willing to commit sexual immorality will appear charming and alluring. She will sweet-talk a man into going to bed with her. She will do all she can to make herself appealing. Yet in the end she's very deadly—"her feet go down to death." That's why the father declares in no uncertain terms:

> Now then, my sons, listen to me and do not depart from the words of my mouth. Keep your way far from her and do not go near the door of her house, or you will give your vigor to others and your years to the cruel one; and strangers will be filled with your strength and your hard-earned goods will go to the house of an alien; and you groan at your final end, when your flesh and your body are consumed; and you say, "How I have hated instruction! And

my heart spurned reproof! I have not listened to the voice of my teachers, nor inclined my ear to my instructors!" (verses 7-13).

He's saying, "Don't give your hard-earned goods to others. Don't give away your seed to someone else and end up supporting children from a woman who isn't yours. Don't give your strength to another family and end up paying alimony for the rest of your life. For if you do, you'll be consumed, and you'll regret what you did. You'll realize how foolish you were." And he doesn't stop there. He goes on:

> My son, observe the commandment of your father and do not forsake the teaching of your mother… for the commandment is a lamp and the teaching is light; and reproofs for discipline are the way of life to keep you from the evil woman, from the smooth tongue of the adulteress. Do not desire her beauty in your heart, nor let her capture you with her eyelids. For on account of a harlot one is reduced to a loaf of bread, and an adulteress hunts for the precious life (Proverbs 6:20,23-26).

An adulterous woman can utterly destroy her prey. A man who succumbs to her will be reduced to nothing. He can lose his wealth, freedom, family, dignity, and even his soul (verse 32).

In case the son foolishly thinks he can get away with indulging his passions, the father warns: "Can a man take fire in his bosom and his clothes not be burned? Or can a man walk on hot coals and his feet not be scorched?" (verses 27-28).

The answer is obvious—*no*, emphatically. "So is the one who goes in to his neighbor's wife; whoever touches her will not go unpunished" (verse 29).

> The one who commits adultery with a woman is
> lacking sense; he who would destroy himself does it.
> Wounds and disgrace will he find, and his reproach
> will not be blotted out (verses 32-33).

So the young man who falls prey to an adulterous woman destroys himself. The stigma that results from his foolishness "will not be blotted out"—that is, it will be permanent. There is a heavy price to pay for letting one's sexual passion run out of control.

Proverbs chapter 7 sounds yet another warning. Note how it describes the man who is enticed by an adulteress: "I saw among the naive, and discerned among the youths a young man lacking sense" (verse 7). In his stupidity, this young man is wandering around in a part of town he shouldn't be in. He's making himself vulnerable to temptation. The adulteress determines he is exactly the kind of man she is looking for— he lacks sense.

This is when the hunt begins. He passes "through the street near her corner; and he takes the way to her house, in the twilight of the evening, in the middle of the night and in the darkness. And behold, a woman comes to meet him, dressed as a harlot and cunning of heart" (verses 8-10). She comes out to greet her victim. Now note her tactics:

> She seizes him and kisses him and with a brazen face
> she says to him: "I was due to offer peace offerings;

today I have paid my vows. Therefore I have come
out to meet you, to seek your presence earnestly, and
I have found you" (verses 13-15).

In other words, "Will you come and help me with my religious celebration? You're just the guy I was looking for." Then
comes the sensual seduction:

I have spread my couch with coverings, with col-
ored linens of Egypt. I have sprinkled my bed with
myrrh, aloes and cinnamon. Come, let us drink our
fill of love until morning; let us delight ourselves with
caresses. For my husband is not at home, he has gone
on a long journey; he has taken a bag of money with
him, at the full moon he will come home (verses
16-20).

Not only does she brazenly invite him to have sex; she says
her husband is gone on a long journey and took a lot of money
with him, which means he won't be back for a while. "With
her flattering lips she seduces him" (verse 21).

Then comes the kill:

Suddenly he follows her as an ox goes to the slaughter,
or as one in fetters to the disciplines of a fool, until
an arrow pierces through his liver; as a bird hastens
to the snare, so he does not know that it will cost him
his life…Her house is the way to Sheol, descending
to the chambers of death (verses 22-23,27).

With such dire consequences, can you see why it's urgent
for fathers to teach their sons to control their own bodies?

Teach your son sexual purity. Tell him to keep his hands to himself. Warn him to stay far away from temptation. Emphasize his need to guard his eyes, his ears, his feet. For when he keeps himself sexually pure, he will avoid the devastating consequences of sexual immorality and be blessed by God.

6. Teach Your Children to Enjoy Their Spouse

While sex is forbidden before or outside of marriage, it is exalted within the marriage union itself. This truth is articulated beautifully in Proverbs chapter 5:

> Drink water from your own cistern and fresh water from your own well. Should your springs be dispersed abroad, streams of water in the streets? Let them be yours alone and not for strangers with you. Let your fountain be blessed, and rejoice in the wife of your youth. As a loving hind and a graceful doe, let her breasts satisfy you at all times; be exhilarated always with her love (verses 15-19).

In other words, a man who is sexually thirsty is to find satisfaction from his own wife. He is to drink from his own cistern, and not spill "streams of water in the streets."

In the ancient Middle East, no one in their right mind would throw buckets of water on the streets. Water was a precious commodity. It was scarce, and it was hard to obtain. So throwing water on the streets was foolish. And the same is true about a man who fathers children all over town.

The statement "let your fountain be blessed" (verse 18) is a reference to a man's procreative capability. He is to rejoice only in the wife of his youth. He is to take pleasure in no one else.

Teach your son, by the way you treat and speak to your wife, to seek fulfillment in his marriage alone. As Proverbs 31:10 says, a wife is a gift from God who is more precious than jewels. She is to be her husband's best friend and companion. He is to enjoy her alone. And the best way to teach that to your son is to enjoy your wife.

7. Teach Your Children to Watch Their Words

Another crucial lesson fathers should teach their children is to be careful about how they speak. Proverbs 4:24 says, "Put away from you a deceitful mouth and put devious speech far from you." Don't speak hypocritically; don't lie. Speak only that which is truthful.

Proverbs 10:11 says, "The mouth of the righteous is a fountain of life." Later in verse 20 we read, "The tongue of the righteous is as choice silver." That is, good words are precious and valuable. Verse 32 adds, "The lips of the righteous bring forth what is acceptable."

Then there are the contrasts—Proverbs 10:14 says, "With the mouth of the foolish, ruin is at hand." Verse 18 states, "He who conceals hatred has lying lips, and he who spreads slander is a fool." So children should be taught not to lie. If they are allowed to get away with lying, the behavior will continue. Teach your children to speak the truth, and make it clear that you will not tolerate lying.

Proverbs also tells us that "when there are many words, transgression is unavoidable, but he who restrains his lips is wise" (10:19). Teach your children to practice self-restraint when they speak. When they keep talking endlessly, they risk saying something they'll regret later on. Help them to choose their words carefully and not stray into slander, gossip, and other foolish speech.

One excellent New Testament passage to share with your children is Ephesians 4:29: "Let no unwholesome word proceed from your mouth, but only such a word as is good for edification according to the need of the moment, so that it will give grace to those who hear." Before they speak, teach your children to ask themselves: Is what I'm about to say edifying? Is it appropriate? Is it gracious? As Christians, our speech should be uplifting, instructive, and helpful. Yes, there will be times when it is necessary to give rebuke or correction. But even that is to be given in a loving, constructive spirit.

8. Teach Your Children to Work Hard

In your role as leader of the family, you are to teach your children how to work. This needs to be done by both word and example. Note what the father in Proverbs tells his son: "Go to the ant…observe her ways and be wise, which, having no chief, officer or ruler, prepares her food in the summer and gathers her provision in the harvest" (6:6-8).

One of the first things you want to teach your children is to do their work diligently even when there is no one supervising them. Even an ant will do that. Of course you can expect your children to work when you're watching them. But what about when no one is around?

If your children are going to be successful in life, they need to be self-motivated to work, as well as plan ahead. They must learn how to labor for their wages, and make provision for their future needs.

The father goes on to say, "How long will you lie down, O sluggard? When will you arise from your sleep? 'A little sleep, a little slumber, a little folding of the hands to rest'—your poverty will come in like a vagabond and your need like an armed man" (verses 9-11). In other words, "You're going to end up poor if you don't learn how to work."

A sluggard is someone who is lazy—he gives excuses for not working, and he procrastinates when it's time to work. According to Proverbs, the lazy person will suffer hunger, poverty, and failure. By contrast, the person who is willing to work hard will earn a living, have the means to obtain food, and will be recognized and rewarded for his efforts. According to Proverbs 22:29, "A man skilled in his work...will stand before kings; he will not stand before obscure men."

Proverbs 10:4-5 sums it up well: "Poor is he who works with a negligent hand, but the hand of the diligent makes rich. He who gathers in summer is a son who acts wisely, but he who sleeps in harvest is a son who acts shamefully."

9. Teach Your Children to Manage Their Money Well

The book of Proverbs speaks often about managing finances because money plays such a big role in life. Much of our time is devoted to earning it. Ironically, however, many people don't take the time necessary to manage it well. If we're careful with our money, we can make it serve some very useful purposes. But if we're careless, money can become the source of much anxiety and heartache.

Here are two key principles from Proverbs you can teach your children so they manage their finances wisely:

Be Generous with God

Proverbs 3:9-10 says, "Honor the LORD from your wealth and from the first of all your produce; so your barns will be filled with plenty and your vats will overflow with new wine." The principle here is that if you are generous with God, He will be generous with you. Typically people view their money as belonging to them, and whatever they give to the Lord is His. But it is God who provides everything we have, and we're to see *all* our money as belonging to Him—not just the portion we place in the offering.

We are called to honor God with the ways we use our money—both the portion given to Him and the portion we spend on ourselves. That's the attitude you want to pass on to your children.

If your kids see that you're a mediocre giver, that's what they'll become too. They're going to learn from your example. And you'll forfeit the promised blessing of God in return. If you want your children to know the fullness of God's blessings, then teach them how to give generously.

Don't Cosign with a Stranger

In Proverbs 6, the father warns, "My son, if you have become surety for your neighbor, have given a pledge for a stranger, if you have been snared with the words of your mouth…Go, humble yourself…deliver yourself like a gazelle from the hunter's hand and like a bird from the hand of the fowler" (verses 1-3,5).

What is this talking about? Suppose a neighbor or stranger comes up to you and says, "I need money to help me with a special project or to get out of debt. I promise that if you help me, I'll give you a big return." The Bible says not to lend money to such a person. When you do, you end up yielding the stewardship of your money to someone for whom you cannot be accountable. You will have released your God-given provision into a financial arrangement you have no control over. Which means you could very well lose your money.

Teach your children to use their money wisely and not become liable for another person whose behavior they cannot control. Warn them that if they cosign with another person, they could become liable for his debts. Far better that your children be able to use their money as the Lord leads, and not have it taken away by someone else in a get-rich-quick scheme that could go wrong and impose a major liability.

If your children do find themselves in that situation, what are they to do? They're to humble themselves and beg to negotiate a settlement so they can back out of the arrangement. They need to do it immediately so they don't get burned financially. They're to do what they can to break free of that bondage and deliver themselves "like a gazelle from the hunter's hand and like a bird from the hand of the fowler" (6:5). In other words, get out!

10. Teach Your Children to Love Their Neighbor

Though Scripture says we should not cosign with a stranger, that doesn't mean we don't give money to someone who is in real need. Proverbs 3:27-28 is clear on this: "Do not withhold good from those to whom it is due, when it is in your power to do it. Do not say to your neighbor, 'Go, and come back, and tomorrow I will give it,' when you have it with you."

If you've got the goods, give to those who are in need.

Being generous with the poor and meeting the needs of others when you have the resources to do so is a part of honoring God. You're to be generous in showing sacrificial love to your neighbor.

Another aspect of loving your neighbor is to not devise harm against him when he lives in security beside you (Proverbs 3:29). The next verse says, "Do not contend with a man without cause, if he has done you no harm." If a neighbor hasn't done anything to you, don't plot to do harm against him. And don't be vengeful—that is the way of the wicked. The curse of the Lord is on such people (verses 31-33).

Take care of your neighbor, love him, forgive him, and meet his needs. As you do so, you "will inherit honor" (verse 35). And your children will imitate you and do the same.

It's well worth noting that Jesus included loving your neighbor as one of the two greatest commandments. When He was asked by a lawyer, "Teacher, which is the great commandment in the Law?" Jesus answered, "'You shall love the Lord your God with all your heart, and with all your soul, and with all your mind.' This is the great and foremost commandment. The second is like it, 'You shall love your neighbor as yourself'" (Matthew 22:36-39). The whole of a person's moral duty, then, comes down to love for God and love for one's neighbor.

What Happens When We Fail to Lead and Teach?

We've just looked at ten crucial lessons you as a father should teach your children, and Proverbs is filled with additional wisdom you can impart to them. These are among the ways you can "bring them up in the discipline and instruction of the Lord" (Ephesians 6:4). Key to making sure your children apply these lessons is that you lead by example. You are to live out your instruction before their eyes so they can emulate you.

When we consider the dangerous consequences of *not* teaching these lessons to our children, it points out all the more the urgency of taking the time to implant biblical truth in their hearts:

- If you fail to teach your children to fear God, the devil will teach them to reject and hate God.

- If you fail to teach your children to guard their minds, the devil will gladly teach them to have an "open mind."

- If you fail to teach your children to obey you and their mother, the devil will teach them to rebel and break your hearts.

- If you fail to teach your children to select their companions carefully, the devil will gladly choose their companions for them.

- If you fail to teach your children to control their bodies, the devil will teach them to give their bodies over to lust.

- If you fail to teach your children to enjoy the marriage partner given to them by God, the devil will teach them how to destroy their marriage through unfaithfulness and adultery.

- If you fail to teach your children to watch their words, the devil will fill their mouths with gossip, slander, lies, and foul language.

- If you fail to teach your children to work hard, the devil will teach them to be lazy, which will impoverish them.

- If you fail to teach your children how to manage their money properly, the devil will teach them to spend it carelessly and go into debt.

- If you fail to teach your children to love their neighbors, the devil will gladly teach them to love only themselves.

As fathers, then, we have a great responsibility to the next generation. How our children turn out has everything to do with the extent of our commitment to teaching them to live according to God's wisdom and truth. May we, as instruments of God's grace, be faithful teachers who lead in the home and bring up our children "in the discipline and instruction of the Lord."

The prodigal father was so lavishly compassionate in his love that he was willing to suffer any humiliation to restore his long-lost son. So many parents do the exact opposite—even Christian parents. When their children start going off in the wrong direction, they speak to them with scorn and treat them with shame. Instead of humbling themselves, they humiliate their children, even to their own destruction. But here Jesus gives fathers and mothers a better model to follow…[12]

PHILIP GRAHAM RYKEN

CHAPTER 5

A Father's Love for a Rebellious Child

We have been looking at what it means for fathers to bring up their children "in the discipline and instruction of the Lord" (Ephesians 6:4). The word "discipline" stresses every father's duty to be a restraint and deterrent to his children's sinful bent—leading them and correcting them lovingly but firmly so that they might obey what is good and avoid what is evil. The word "instruction" points to a positive duty to guide them in the way of biblical wisdom. The first priority here is to cultivate in our children a healthy fear of God, a humble understanding of their own guilt, and a sense of their need for Christ as their Savior. From there we can teach them to live by the truth of Scripture, encourage their love of God, and steer them in a righteous direction so that they might grow to spiritual maturity.

We've also seen that, according to Deuteronomy 6:7, the father's job is constant. It is not a part-time role, and there is no time off. We're to talk about the Lord with our children day in and day out, when we sit down and when we rise up.

Everything we have covered up to this point assumes that your children are still teachable—that they're willing to listen, that they are receptive to your efforts to pass on a biblical legacy to them.

But what if you already have one or more children who are living in staunch rebellion against you? What if your parental authority has been rejected? What are you to do when a child refuses to cooperate or goes so far as to reject the Christian faith or leave the home?

In such situations, how is a father to respond?

Because there are so many possible scenarios when it comes to childhood rebellion, rather than attempt to address the variables, I'd like to focus on the kind of *heart attitude* a father is to have in the face of such rejection. That is the starting point for any father who needs to equip himself to deal with a rebellious child. There are other helpful resources a Christian parent can turn to with regard to specifics, and I've listed a couple of them in the endnotes for this chapter on page 143.[13]

So what heart attitude should you have when your children become stubborn or, even worse, reject you outright? We find this attitude beautifully illustrated for us in what is commonly known as the parable of the prodigal son. In this story, told by Jesus in Luke chapter 15, we see a father whose son expresses the most complete sort of rejection imaginable. The son shows utter disregard and contempt for his father, spurns his family, and departs for a faraway land to squander the family wealth on reckless living.

The father in this story is representative of God Himself. And as we go through the parable, note carefully his heart attitude toward his son, for this is exactly the same attitude God displays toward rebellious sinners. It is this kind of heart that you as a father need to demonstrate toward a child who has chosen to reject your parental guidance.

The parable of the prodigal son has three basic parts that overlap. The first part is about the younger son. The second part is about the father. And the third is about the older son. For the purposes of this chapter, we're going to focus on the second part and see how the father responds to his rebellious younger son. But to get the full context, we'll start at the beginning of the parable:

> A man had two sons. The younger of them said to his father, "Father, give me the share of the estate that falls to me." So he divided his wealth between them. And not many days later, the younger son gathered everything together and went on a journey into a distant country, and there he squandered his estate with loose living. Now when he had spent everything, a severe famine occurred in that country, and he began to be impoverished. So he went and hired himself out to one of the citizens of that country, and he sent him into his fields to feed swine. And he would have gladly filled his stomach with the pods that the swine were eating, and no one was giving anything to him (verses 11-16).

The Outrageous Demand

To fully appreciate what takes place in the story, it's necessary to understand some of the cultural norms of the ancient Middle East. Typically, children were not entitled to any inheritance while their father was still alive. But here, the younger son insists on receiving his share of the estate immediately. It's an outrageous, shameless request because it's tantamount to saying, "Dad, I wish you were dead. I want what is mine, and I want it now."

Then the son gathered his belongings and went on a journey to a distant country, where he wasted his father's money on "loose living" (verse 13). The Greek term for "loose" means "dissolute" or "wasteful" (that's what the older word *prodigal* actually means) and speaks of a reckless, debauched lifestyle. After the son runs out of money, he has no choice but to take on a job, and the only one he can find is that of feeding swine. This is the worst sort of degradation possible for a man of Jewish heritage, for pigs were considered unclean animals.

In summary, this young man illustrates someone who has gone as low as it is possible to go. He's living in outrageous immorality and residing as a Jewish man in a Gentile country among unclean pigs. And he is so destitute that he would have eaten the pigs' food if he could. In the minds of the Jews in the ancient Middle East, it would be impossible to imagine an uglier, more desperate scenario.

The Beginning of Repentance

It is at this point that the son "came to his senses." He said, "How many of my father's hired men have more than enough bread, but I am dying here with hunger!" (verse 17). We can expect that he had done everything he could to keep his father out of mind while he was indulging himself in his debauched lifestyle. But now he is left with nothing. There is a famine in the land, and he is dying of hunger. It's not until he reaches this point that he wakes up to the reality of where sin has led him, and he finally begins thinking more sensibly.

What's interesting here is that the young man's father comes to his mind. It is at this time that we see the beginning of repentance, which starts with a sinner's accurate assessment of his condition. The son comes to realize he has no resources to get out of the predicament he's in. He is dying of hunger, and no one will give anything to him. All this drives the son to honestly evaluate where he stands. And that, in turn, brings him to the beginning of repentance.

The Generosity of the Father

The son's first thought is, "How many of my father's hired men have more than enough bread, but I am dying here with hunger!" (verse 17). His observation tells us a lot about his father. Back in those days, a hired man was a day laborer. These laborers were at the lowest level of the social ladder. They were basically poor people who were, for the most part, unskilled. They usually worked on a day-to-day basis. They did temporary jobs for others, such as harvesting crops. They earned very meager wages that gave them barely enough to survive.

So what does the son remember about his father? That he paid his laborers more than enough. That is to say, his father was generous. He gave his workers more than the minimum needed to survive. This indicates he was loving, kind, and generous. Clearly he observed the Old Testament law which mandated that the wages of a hired man were not to remain with you all night until morning (Leviticus 19:13). If you hired someone to work for you and he ate on the basis of that work and needed money to sustain him and his family, you were to pay him on the day he did the work.

That the father did more than what the Old Testament law required reveals that he is generous. This is what the son remembers. He acknowledges that his father is not a hard or indifferent man. His father is kind; he has seen this with his own eyes. He doesn't know anyone else like that, and he has nowhere else to turn.

It would be easy for us to assume that because the father had been so totally disgraced and dishonored by his son in such a public manner, he wouldn't want him back at all. That's certainly the perspective Jesus' listeners would have had. But the son knows his father better than that. He knows his father is not vengeful, but merciful and gracious.

The Dilemma Facing the Son

We gain more insight about the situation of hired workers in those days from Jesus' story about the harvesters in Matthew 20. There, we read about a landowner who "went out early in the morning to hire laborers for his vineyard" (verse 1). He struck a deal to pay each worker a denarius for the day's work. He then went out again at 9:00 a.m., 12:00 p.m., and 3:00 p.m. to hire more workers. At the end of the day, he paid every one of them a denarius, regardless of how long they had labored. Ultimately, day workers were not in a position to negotiate—they were at the mercy of the terms set by the person who hired them.

In fact, day laborers were even lower on the ladder than

slaves. That's because slaves lived with the family, were part of the household, and had their food, lodging, and other needs provided for. Even though they usually weren't paid any wages, they were cared for. By contrast, hired men were on their own. They took what they could get to survive.

The prodigal son's father, however, was generous with his workers. And because the son had no other alternatives, he decided he was ready to return. All he could do was humble himself, face his shame, and admit his terrible sin. His hope was that he would be treated with the same kind of compassion he knew his father showed to poor people. There's no hint that the son had any hope of regaining his father's approval or goodwill. He certainly had no right to *expect* any kind of favor. Nor would he ever be able to earn back what he had squandered from his father's wealth and beneficence. His best and only hope now was to be a hired

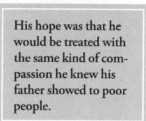

His hope was that he would be treated with the same kind of compassion he knew his father showed to poor people.

laborer in his father's fields. At least he would have steady work, and he would not be subject to the abuse and starvation he had encountered in a far-off land.

Of course, the people who were listening to Jesus tell this parable understood all this. They would have said, "Yes, if the son is truly repentant, he will go back to his father, confess his sin, and humbly apologize. He deserves to be humiliated and scorned, and that's only fair because of how horribly he treated his father." These people lived in an honor/shame culture that taught it was very important to protect the honor of elders. They exhibited a harsh, severe attitude toward children who disgraced their parents. Even if the son was repentant and humbly willing do whatever was necessary to make restitution possible, Jesus' listeners fully expected the father would treat his son as an outcast upon his return. The son deserved every bit of humiliation and punishment that would come from the hand of his father.

The Marks of a Repentant Heart

In the son's brokenness we see the penitent heart of a sinner who is ready to turn his life around. It is only when the heart is destitute that a person sees his need for salvation. And the son expresses not only a willingness to repent, but faith in his father—here we see repentance linked with faith. The son trusts what he has seen of his father's goodness, compassion, and generosity. In spite of the horrible way he has dishonored and shamed his father, he knows his father is a forgiving man. He is ready to go back and ask for forgiveness and accept the consequences of his sin.

Upon deciding he would return home, the young man began to rehearse what he would say. "Father, I have sinned against heaven, and in your sight; I am no longer worthy to be called your son; make me as one of your hired men" (verses 18-19).

No doubt at this point of Jesus' storytelling the self-righteous Jewish religious leaders in the crowd were all nodding with approval and saying, "That's exactly what the son needs to do. He must put himself at the mercy of his father, and ask for permission to work as a hired hand. He must place himself at the lowest point of the social ladder without any kind of relationship with his father—not even the kind that would be enjoyed by a slave, let alone a son. After all, he has no right to go home."

In that culture, what the son was about to do was profoundly humbling, embarrassing in the extreme, and saturated with the odium of public shame. But the prodigal determined that he would follow through. In fact, listen to how severe he is in his self-indictment: "I have sinned against heaven, and in your sight" (verse 18). The original Greek text here could be taken to mean, "My sins pile up as high as heaven." The son realized the magnitude of his wrongdoing. We find a similar spirit of repentance in a prayer of intercession spoken by Ezra some centuries earlier on behalf of Israel: "O my God, I am ashamed and embarrassed to lift up my face to You, my God, for our iniquities have risen above our heads and our guilt has grown even to the heavens" (Ezra 9:6).

In the son's confession, we find the mark of true repentance. He was saying, "My life has been a total disaster. I am facing death, and there is no one to blame but myself. I rebelled; I wasted my life, I dishonored my father. My sins stack so high they rise to the very presence of God." True repentance holds nothing back and offers no excuses. That's how it is with repentance—the sinner is struck with an overwhelming conviction regarding his or her own condition.

As the son rehearsed the speech he would give to his father, he was clearly convinced he deserved permanent exclusion from his family and a lifetime of humiliation and lowly work.

But he was so fed up with his sin and so humbled by sin's consequences that he was returning home to face the music with an attitude that was the polar opposite of the arrogant swagger he displayed when he left.

Clearly, this was true remorse. The glitter and allure of the far country was long gone. The freewheeling lifestyle he had enjoyed had turned into a terrible, crushing bondage. His dreams had turned to nightmares; his pleasure had turned to pain; the fun had turned to sorrow; the self-fulfillment had turned to self-deprivation. The party was over for good. The laughs had long since died out and his friends were all gone. He had finally come to the end of himself.

This is not to say that every sinner waits until he has reached absolute rock bottom before he repents. That was not Jesus' point. Rather, Jesus wanted to emphasize the nature of the father's response to his son, which we will see in a moment. Jesus wanted to make it clear that even though the son had committed the worst possible offenses against his father, the father was still willing to extend full forgiveness to him. This would tell Jesus' listeners that if God can completely forgive even the worst of sinners, then there is hope for everyone who repents, no matter how vile the person's sin.

The Unexpected Turn of Events

What happens next is startling:

> So he got up and came to his father. But while he was still a long way off, his father saw him and felt compassion for him, and ran and embraced him and kissed him (verse 20).

At this point, if the self-righteous Jewish religious leaders were standing, they probably fell over in shock. They couldn't believe what Jesus had just said. This was way beyond their sensibilities.

After all, the son had acted shamefully and justice demanded punishment. Furthermore, the boy had done nothing to earn the servant's status he was asking for; much less did he deserve immediate forgiveness. And full reconciliation would seem out of the question forever. According to the customs of the time, the father had every right to refuse to meet with his son, and to make him sit outside the gate of the family home for days in public view while the townspeople heaped scorn on him. Then when the father finally opened the gate, the son would be required to bow low and kiss his father's feet. At which time the father would tell him, in a stern manner, what works he would have to do to prove that his repentance was real. Then, and only then, could his request to serve as a hired laborer be granted. That's what the Jewish rabbis taught—restitution had to be paid, and mercy needed to be earned.

The Father's Watchful Anticipation

But that is not what happened. In fact, in the minds of Jesus' listeners, what took place could only be described as scandalous: "While [the son] was still a long way off, his father saw him and felt compassion for him, and ran and embraced him and kissed him" (verse 20). The father had the nerve to *run* all the way to his son. Obviously, for the father to see the boy while he was still in the far-off distance, he must have been anxiously, constantly watching for his son. This gives us some insight into how much the father loved his son.

Picture the scene: It's daylight, the father sees his son in the distance, and he runs. Because this happens during the day, the town would have been bustling with people. It would have been full of women and children and older people and anyone else who wasn't out working in the surrounding fields. So the father ran in full view of all these people. And they're shocked at his behavior.

The Father's Loving Protection

Why did the father run? Very simply, he wanted to reach his son before the son got to the village. The father not only wanted to initiate reconciliation in the same way as the shepherd who found the lost sheep and the woman who found the lost coin (Luke 15:1-10), he wanted to reach his son first before the townspeople could heap abuse upon him. The father was willing to take that scorn on behalf of his son. He was willing to let people say, "What is this father doing? He has been dishonored, and now he dishonors himself even more by embracing his wretched son." The father knew what the cultural expectations were, but he didn't care. He wanted to protect his son.

This becomes more apparent when we note that the father "felt compassion" for his son (verse 20). Not just compassion over his son's past sin or present filth, but for what the son was in danger of experiencing when he arrived in the village. The Greek term translated "compassion" comes from a root word that refers to the intestines, the bowels, the abdomen. The father felt a sick feeling in his stomach when he saw his son and realized the scorn and anger that everyone would heap upon him. So he ran to protect him.

The Father's Willingness to Embarrass Himself

Why were the villagers so shocked when they saw the father running? Because in the ancient Middle East, noblemen didn't run. It was undignified. A man of means hired runners to deliver messages and do errands for him. He himself always walked upright in a stately manner. To run he would have to hold up the hem of his robe and expose the calves of his legs. It made him look silly, immature, lacking composure. No honorable man would do that in public—especially under these circumstances, welcoming a son who had so severely shamed him. It simply wasn't done. In fact, this was such a deeply engrained part of Middle Eastern culture that for centuries, Arabic translations of the Bible did not say the father ran. It's as if the translators wanted to avoid this humiliating truth.

The word translated "ran" is a form of the Greek verb *trecho*, which speaks of running a race. This is a full-fledged sprint. It's as if the father is impatient and cannot get to his son fast enough. He didn't just jog or shuffle along. He raced toward his son at top speed.

So the father, in running to his son, brings shame and scorn upon himself, violating fundamental cultural expectations. He is willing to embarrass himself to protect his son from embarrassment. He risks the mockery and slander of his fellow villagers so his son doesn't have to bear it. And when the father reaches his son, even more shockingly, he embraces him. He falls on his son's neck, gives him a big hug, and kisses him (verse 20). He does this even though the son is filthy, his clothes are ragged, and he is no doubt covered with the stench of pigs. This extraordinary reception tells us the father had been suffering silently over his son the entire time he was gone. And now his immense love for the boy was put on very public display.

By this time Jesus' listeners had to have been completely aghast. All this affection from the father was being showered on the prodigal son before he even had an opportunity to begin his carefully rehearsed confession to the father. This wasn't the kind of welcome Jesus' listeners expected!

A Picture of God's Love for Sinners

You want to know how eager God is to receive a sinner? We see it here in the way the father greeted his son. God will run through the dirt and bear the shame. He will embrace the sinner with all His strength and kiss him. Some people view God as a reluctant Savior. He's not. All heaven rejoices when a person repents and seeks His forgiveness.

> Some people view God as a reluctant Savior. He's not.

This unexpected turn in Jesus' story was totally unorthodox. It went against everything that culture taught. The father had publicly humiliated himself out of a deep love for his son. He had run through the dirt of the village to protect his son from everyone's scorn and shame. And he had embraced his son and kissed him even as he still wore filthy, ragged clothing. This father was doing exactly what Jesus did on our behalf. Jesus came into our village to run the gauntlet and bear the shame and throw His arms around us and kiss us and reconcile us to Him.

A Picture of Salvation by Grace

Jesus' listeners were further stunned by the fact the father showered his son with love and without requiring any works or restitution from him. Notice what happened when the son began to deliver the speech he had rehearsed: "I have sinned against heaven, and in your sight; I am no longer worthy to be called your son" (verse 21). Before he could say, "Make me as one of your hired men" (verse 19), the father interrupted with a rapid-fire series of instructions to his slaves.

A Picture of Full Restoration

The full extent of the father's forgiveness is made clear by what he says when he interrupts the son's confession. His objective, clearly, is not merely to show the son a modicum of mercy. He will not only grant the repentant prodigal full forgiveness and restoration; he fully intends to *honor* this son who had shamed him!

> The father said to his slaves, "Quickly bring out the best robe and put it on him, and put a ring on his hand and sandals on his feet; and bring the fattened calf, kill it, and let us eat and celebrate; for this son of mine was dead and has come to life again; he was lost and has been found." And they began to celebrate (verses 22-24).

There is tremendous symbolic significance here. The fact the father gave his son a robe, a ring, and sandals had very clear meaning to the crowd listening to this parable. In those days, every nobleman owned a finely crafted robe that was set aside for only the most special occasions. The Greek term used here means "first-ranking garment." In putting this robe on his son, the father was bestowing incredibly great honor on him. What's more, the father did this even though his son was still covered with dirt and filth!

Next, the father put a ring on his son's hand. This would have been a signet ring that bore the family crest or seal. Such rings were used to press the family insignia on the wax seals placed on official documents. Thus the ring was a symbol of authority. The father had bestowed his own authority upon the son.

And finally, sandals were placed on the son's feet. Back then, sandals were usually worn by masters and their sons, and not by slaves or hired laborers. This signified that the father had fully restored the young man's place as his son.

The robe, ring, and sandals were ways of saying, "The best of everything I have is yours. You have been fully restored as my son." The full rights and privileges of sonship had been returned to the young man. In showering his son with forgiveness, the father held nothing back.

So of course Jesus' listeners were astounded. This father was defying many of the strict cultural customs and expectations of the day. He had no concerns whatsoever about his own honor. In fact, he showered honors on a son who wasn't deserving of any favor at all. All of this greatly confused the crowd. Their perception was that a sinner needed to earn God's favor through works and the law. Jesus was illustrating the principle of Ephesians 2:8-9: "By grace you have been saved through faith; and that not of yourselves, it is the gift of

God; not as a result of works, so that no one may boast." And Titus 3:5-7: "He saved us, not on the basis of deeds which we have done in righteousness, but according to His mercy, by the washing of regeneration and renewing by the Holy Spirit, whom He poured out upon us richly through Jesus Christ our Savior, so that being justified by His grace we would be made heirs according to the hope of eternal life."

There's even more symbolic meaning behind the gifts the father bestowed upon his younger son. Traditionally, in that culture, the robe and ring would have gone to the elder son. Or, the father would have saved the robe to wear at his eldest son's wedding. In those days, the marriage of the eldest son was the biggest celebratory event that could happen in a family. And the ring, signifying the legal authority to carry out official business for the family, would have gone to him as well. Because the younger son had already spent his portion of the inheritance, everything that was still left would have gone to the older son.

Yet the father, because he was still alive and the patriarch of the family, could do whatever he wanted with the possessions that, technically speaking, were still his. In placing the robe, ring, and sandals on his younger son, he sent a clear message to everyone in the village: The young man had gained back every privilege to be enjoyed by a nobleman's son. He had full access to the family treasures again. He had been fully forgiven, and reconciliation was immediate and complete. There would be no waiting period during which the son was expected to prove himself through hard work.

The son came to his father with nothing to offer. He had

recognized his utterly destitute state. He hadn't come with a suitcase in his hand. That's how it is when a sinner comes to God with a repentant heart. Whom does God justify? "The one who does not work, but believes in Him who justifies the ungodly" (Romans 4:5). God forgives those who come to Him empty-handed. A person cannot earn his way into God's forgiveness and grace.

What is Jesus' message here? Grace triumphs over sin even at its worst. The story isn't that every sinner falls to such great depths of desperation. Rather, it's that grace can cover our sins. It's about undeserved forgiveness, undeserved sonship, undeserved salvation, and undeserved honor without any restitution or works. Such lavish love and grace bestowed upon a penitent, trusting sinner is remarkable. It doesn't fit with the expectations of a legalistic culture.

A Picture of the Joy Expressed When a Sinner Repents

The father then called for a great party:

> "Bring the fattened calf, kill it, and let us eat and cele-
> brate; for this son of mine was dead and has come to
> life again; he was lost and has been found." And they
> began to celebrate (Luke 15:23-24).

Back then, noble families would set aside a calf that would be fattened for a truly special occasion, such as a wedding or the visit of an important dignitary. The father was so overjoyed at his son's return that he treated it as if it were the biggest event that had ever happened in the history of the family or the village. A fattened calf was able to feed a large number of people—as many as 200 or more—so the father may have invited the entire village to celebrate with him.

In this celebration we see a picture of the rejoicing that takes place in heaven over one sinner who repents (Luke 15:7). In fact, earlier in Luke 15, the shepherd who found his lost sheep said to his friends and neighbors, "Rejoice with me, for I have found my sheep which was lost!" (verse 6). And the woman who found her lost coin called together her friends and neighbors and said, "Rejoice with me, for I have found the coin which I had lost!" (verse 9). Here, the father called the whole village to rejoice with him over his son, who had returned home. He said, "Let us eat and celebrate; for this son of mine was dead and has come to life again; he was lost and has been found" (verses 23-24).

What did the father mean when he said, "This son of mine was dead"? When the son had departed for a far country, he had done so in complete rejection of his father and family. Therefore it was highly unlikely he would ever return. So the family probably reckoned him as dead, and in that culture, sometimes a funeral service was conducted in such a scenario. But now that the son was back, he had "come to life." And consistent with the gospel message, the son didn't earn his life back. Rather, his father freely gave him the full rights and privileges of sonship. It was the father who embraced him, kissed him, and restored him as a son.

This celebration, then, wasn't so much for what the son had done as what the father had done. It was the father who restored the son to blessing through merciful forgiveness and gracious love. He exhibited unheard-of kindness, sacrificial love, and abounding grace. The son who was essentially dead was now alive and enjoyed a real relationship with his father, who made him heir of everything he possessed. The son entrusted his life to the father, and the father entrusted his resources to the son, who is now in the father's house. That's how it is with those of us who are followers of Christ.

God receives the sinner who comes to Him in repentance and belief. In John 6:37, Jesus said, "The one who comes to Me I will certainly not cast out." God's forgiving grace is lavish. He replaces the sinner's filthy rags with His own robe of righteousness. He gives us honor, respect, authority, full access to His treasures, and full right to represent Him. As 2 Corinthians 5:20 says, we are His ambassadors.

God is not a reluctant Savior. He runs to embrace and kiss us. He treats us as if we were royalty and hurries to put on the robe, the ring, and the sandals. And He calls all who dwell in heaven to come and celebrate with Him when a sinner is reconciled. He does this every time a sinner repents!

Following God's Example

So how does this apply to you as a father? The parable of the lost son provides a vivid demonstration of the kind of love you are to exhibit toward a rebellious child. This isn't to say you are to condone wrong behavior while it is going on. But you need to stand ready to show forgiveness and grace the whole time you wait for your child to come back to his senses with a repentant heart. You must exhibit a Christlike love as you wait for that to happen. Be patient and show kindness. Follow the example of God's abounding love for sinners.

Those who heard Jesus tell the story thought the younger son should be held accountable for the shameful way he treated his father. They expected the son would have to work hard to earn his way back into the family. Likewise, our human inclination is to hold grudges against our children when they break our hearts. When they make life painful for us, our tendency is to get back at them in some way and make them pay for what they've done.

But that's not how our heavenly Father treated us when we came to Him for forgiveness. He welcomed us with open arms. He poured out His grace and mercy upon us immediately. He is an eager Savior, not a reluctant one.

This heart attitude doesn't apply only to children who reject our parental authority in some substantial way, as happened with the young man in Luke 15. We as parents need to exhibit it even in cases of temporary rebellion. No matter what the situation, when the child becomes repentant, it's time to show the same abounding grace we received from God Himself when we came to Him for salvation. And it's time to remember and be grateful for God's incredible goodness to us.

[Courage] is not from nature but from grace, it is a gift of God; it is he that gives strength and power to his people, not bodily strength only, but spiritual strength; it is he that girds them with strength, with a holy fortitude, and fills them with spiritual courage, and strengthens their hearts, and fortifies them against their spiritual enemies.[14]

JOHN GILL

CHAPTER 6

A Call for Strong and Courageous Dads

I t is remarkable how much emphasis there is in the Bible on the subject of leadership. In fact, from the very beginning of creation, God established in the human realm the need for leadership. In the first marriage, which was between Adam and Eve, God appointed Adam as the leader. And as God's redemptive plan unfolds all through the pages of Scripture, we see not only husbands and fathers who were leaders for their families, but patriarchs, prophets, priests, judges, kings, and military leaders who were chosen or served as leaders for other human institutions of varying sizes, including whole nations.

Then in the pages of the New Testament we come to the greatest leader of all, Jesus Christ. Upon beginning His official ministry, Jesus chose 12 men whom He would train to carry on His work after He ascended to heaven. And they, with the help of the indwelling Holy Spirit, were to train still more leaders for the church so that the process might continue on through the centuries to today. This is one of the primary responsibilities of a leader—bringing up future generations of leaders. The apostle Paul charged Timothy with this task when he said, "The things which you have heard from me in the presence of many witnesses, entrust these to faithful men who will be able to teach others also" (2 Timothy 2:2).

The most foundational form of leadership for all society, however, is the husband's and father's leadership in the home. Beginning with Adam and Eve, God designed the marital relationship between man and woman as the first human institution, and thus it is the most basic building block of society. By order of creation, because Adam was created first and Eve was created as his helper (Genesis 2:18; 1 Corinthians 11:3; Ephesians 5:22-33), the man was vested with the headship of the marriage relationship and the family. As we saw earlier in this book, he is to carry out that leadership role by showing Christlike love for his wife and bringing up his children in the discipline and instruction of the Lord. Ultimately, it is the father's leadership in the home that

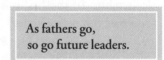

As fathers go,
so go future leaders.

influences, in a very significant way, the kind of future leaders we have in society. As fathers go, so go future leaders. That makes strong leadership in the home crucial.

As we've already seen, when it comes to children, the father's highest priority is *spiritual* leadership.

With that in mind, whenever Scripture presents the principles of good spiritual leadership, there is much that fathers can learn about providing good leadership in the home. In fact, there are times when the Bible speaks of a spiritual leader's responsibilities as being like those of a father. So it shouldn't surprise us that many of the principles for good spiritual leadership are also the same principles of being a good father.

The apostle Paul compared his own spiritual leadership in the church to the work that parents do in the home. From Paul's illustrations in this passage we can learn some valuable lessons about how fathers are to fulfill the calling God has given them.

Church Leadership Is Analogous to Parenting

In 1 Thessalonians 2:7-12, Paul spoke to the Christians at Thessalonica about the kind of leadership he and his fellow ministers exhibited during their stay in the city. What's particularly interesting is that he compared their manner of leadership to the manner of care that a mother and father would give to their children:

> We proved to be gentle among you, *as a nursing mother* tenderly cares for her own children. Having so fond an affection for you, we were well-pleased to impart to you not only the gospel of God but also our own lives, because you had become very dear to us...

> You are witnesses, and so is God, how devoutly and uprightly and blamelessly we behaved toward you believers; just as you know how we were exhorting and encouraging and imploring each one of you *as a father* would his own children, so that you would walk in a manner worthy of the God who calls you into His own kingdom and glory (verses 7-8,10-12, emphases added).

So here Paul chose to illustrate his spiritual leadership as being parental in nature. Elsewhere in the New Testament, we find other pictures used in reference to spiritual leaders—they are portrayed as shepherds (1 Peter 5:1-4), stewards (1 Corinthians 4:1-2), heralds (1 Timothy 2:7), teachers (2 Timothy 2:2), and even slaves (1 Corinthians 3:5-9). Every one of these metaphors is loaded with meaning and emphasizes a certain aspect of spiritual leadership.

In 1 Thessalonians 2:7-12, the metaphors Paul chose were those of a mother and father. He used the picture of a mother to illustrate gentle care, and he used the picture of a father to illustrate strong authority. Those in spiritual leadership are to exemplify both qualities toward those whom they lead. What makes Paul's illustrations so powerful is that everyone can understand what a mother and father's care ought to look like. These are metaphors everyone comprehends.

So in looking at 1 Thessalonians 2:10-12, where Paul spoke of himself "as a father," we who are fathers will find a useful portrait of the kind of leadership we are to demonstrate in the home. While Paul's intent in this passage is to describe the kind of spiritual leadership he provided to the church in Thessalonica, we'll find it instructive with regard to our role as fathers.

What Makes a Man a Man?

If we were to ask people what they believe is the most basic virtue of manliness, we would get many different answers. Our society has all sorts of expectations and perceptions about what a man should be—and much of it is contradictory or confusing. That's why it is helpful to turn to the Bible and see what it says. And in fact, we find a rather interesting statement from the apostle Paul in 1 Corinthians 16 that gives us the answer we're looking for.

If you know anything about the New Testament church in Corinth, you'll remember it was a church given over to compromise. The members were spiritually weak and tolerated sin in their own lives and the lives of others. After addressing these problems, Paul concluded the book of 1 Corinthians with this exhortation:

> Be on the alert, stand firm in the faith, act like men,
> be strong (16:13).

Today when we look at how men act, we see a broad range of behaviors. Especially prevalent is the way men are portrayed on many television shows—they're lazy, dim-witted, uncultured, and generally inept as husbands and fathers. Then there are those who wish to obliterate the God-given distinctions between men and women by telling men they should "get more in touch with their feminine side." But that kind of faulty human wisdom only diminishes the unique character qualities that God designed for a man to use for the good of the family, the home, the workplace, and more.

So how are men to act? Paul gives a direct answer in 1 Corinthians 16:13: "Act like men, be strong."

It's worth noting that the Greek verb translated "act" means "to conduct yourself in a courageous way." The idea here is that men are to have courage and show strength. In the context of the book of 1 Corinthians, Paul was urging his readers to have strength of conviction and have the courage to stand on it.

That is the most basic virtue of manliness. This is what you as a father are to provide in your home—courage and strength. You are to stand strong on your convictions such that you provide certainty, confidence, and stability in the home.

Too many men today are weak, depressed, defeated. They vacillate when it comes to spiritual convictions. As a consequence, they fail to offer the kind of leadership and guidance that a family so desperately needs in today's world.

A father is to face life with courage. He is to believe certain truths and take a stand on them. He is called to fulfill certain responsibilities and to carry them out no matter what kind of opposition he faces. He is to do what Scripture says is right, even though it means paying a price. He is to make the hard decisions that need to be made rather than drift aimlessly in whatever direction today's culture will take him. These are the things that make a man a man. And they make him the kind of father his children need so they can grow up "in the discipline and instruction of the Lord" (Ephesians 6:4).

Be Strong and Courageous

The Greek phrase translated "act like men" in 1 Corinthians 16:13 doesn't appear anywhere else in the New Testament, but we find it present in the Greek translation of the Old Testament, otherwise known as the Septuagint. It appears in Deuteronomy 31, where we find Moses, who is 120 years old, speaking to the nation of Israel and preparing to turn the reins of leadership over to Joshua. As Moses speaks to the people in preparation for their entrance into the Promised Land, he says, "Be strong and courageous." The terminology here, in the Septuagint, is the same as that found in 1 Corinthians 16:13. Moses continues:

> Be strong and courageous, do not be afraid or trem-
> ble at them, for the LORD your God is the one who
> goes with you. He will not fail you or forsake you
> (verse 6).

Then Moses turns to Joshua and says to him, in front of all Israel, "Be strong and courageous" (verse 7). This is how men are to act. They're to be strong, courageous, decisive, and have strength of conviction and virtue. They're to have the kind of courage that refuses to compromise or back down.

We find a similar admonition in 1 Kings 2:2. The context is rather fascinating—King David is giving a final charge to his son Solomon before he dies. These are among his last words. What was the most important thing he could say to Solomon at this time? "I am going the way of all the earth. Be strong, therefore, and show yourself a man."

The next verse tells how Solomon was to fulfill this duty: "Keep the charge of the LORD your God, to walk in His ways, to keep His statutes, His commandments, His ordinances, and His testimonies...that you may succeed in all that you do and wherever you turn" (verse 3). So here we come to see that being strong requires walking in God's ways and com-mands. That's what it means to be a man—to be strong and courageous in the ways of the Lord.

That's the kind of leadership you are to provide for your family. You are called to be strong in your faith, strong in the things of God. You are to provide clear direction to your children about how they are to live. And all of this will require that you be strong and courageous, for you are sure to face opposition. When that happens, your family needs you to stand firm and not waver. Don't succumb to the world's attacks and become weak, intimidated, or dismayed. It's your responsibility to provide the kind of bold leadership that leads your children to develop a similar courage and strength of conviction in their own lives.

> That's what it means to be a man—to be strong and courageous in the ways of the Lord.

The Source of a Godly Man's Strength

Where is a man to find the fortitude to face difficult challenges, contend with life's problems, and press toward the goal? How is he to summon up this courage and strength?

When it came time for Joshua to take the nation of Israel into the Promised Land and do battle, the Lord repeatedly urged him, "Be strong and courageous" (Joshua 1:6), "be strong and very courageous" (verse 7), and "Have I not commanded you? Be strong and courageous!" (verse 9).

But where was Joshua to find this strength and courage?

The Assurance of God's Presence

First, note what God promised to Joshua when He gave His commands: "Just as I have been with Moses, I will be with you; I will not fail you or forsake you" (verse 5). Then again in verse 9 God said, "Do not tremble or be dismayed, for the Lord your God is with you wherever you go."

The first thing that gives a man courage in spiritual leadership is the presence of God. "I'm with you," He says. "I won't leave you, and I won't fail you."

The Pursuit of a Just Cause

Second, after God told Joshua to be strong and courageous, He said, "You shall give this people possession of the land which I swore to their fathers to give them" (verse 6). God had already promised this land to the people of Israel. He would help them in their conquest of it. What they were about to do was according to God's plan, so they had nothing to fear. They were involved in a just cause.

When it comes to how we live, God gives clear instruction in the Scriptures. As Psalm 119:105 says, "Your word is a lamp to my feet and a light to my path." When God calls us to a specific action and we obey, we can move forward with the confidence we are pursuing a just cause. The knowledge we are doing what is right gives us strength and courage.

The Promise of God's Sovereign Power

Third, God told Joshua, "Be careful to do according to all the law which Moses My servant commanded you; do not turn from it to the right or to the left, so that you may have success wherever you go" (Joshua 1:7). Verse 8 expands upon that, saying, "This book of the law shall not depart from your mouth, but you shall meditate on it day and night, so that you may be careful to do according to all that is written in it; for then you will make your way prosperous, and then you will have success."

God promised that when Joshua remained steadfast in His law, He would bless Joshua and give him success. God was able to make such a promise because He is fully sovereign and has control over all things. When we are faithful to follow God's Word, God assures us of success. This success, of course, is made possible by God's sovereign power.

Courage in spiritual leadership, then, comes from the assurance of God's presence, the pursuit of right causes, and the promise of God's sovereign power over all things.

When Opposition Comes

Some people will say, "But what about those times when a Christian stands strong on his convictions and gets in trouble for it? Isn't that a problem?" No, it's not if we've already determined that what we're doing is right and biblical. If we're living in accord with God's commands, we can have assurance He is with us and promises us His kind of success. In the eyes of the world we may be failing. We may be going against the grain. But from God's perspective, we're doing the right thing.

That's the kind of conviction a spiritual leader should have. And by virtue of the fact the father is the spiritual leader of the home, it's the kind of conviction you must have as well. You are to be decisive, bold, strong, and courageous with regard to what you believe and live for.

If you want to raise your children "in the discipline and instruction of the Lord" (Ephesians 6:4), you need to set the standard in your home. You need to be an example of strength and courage. If you live boldly by God's Word without compromise and resist the pressure to please men, then you'll lead your children to live in the same way. Don't sell out integrity for comfort. Don't be afraid of what others might think. Seek to please God and hold to your convictions so that you will fulfill the leadership role God has called you to in your home.

That is what it means to act like a man.

What a Father's Leadership Looks Like

Now let's return to 1 Thessalonians 2 and look at Paul's portrait of spiritual leaders as fathers.

The Character of a Father's Leadership

The larger context of Paul's words in 1 Thessalonians 2:7-12 is that there were detractors who, after Paul left town, claimed that Paul was no different from the fake religious teachers that had plagued the church. He was just another charlatan and fraud who wanted to manipulate the people, get their money, and take advantage of them.

Paul responds to those charges by reminding the Christians in Thessalonica of the authenticity of his leadership. In essence, he writes, "Please remember what you know to be true about me. You know I wasn't a fake, and you know I took nothing from you." Then Paul goes on to validate the character of his spiritual leadership by reminding the Thessalonians of the way he lived among them. It's at this point he portrays his leadership as being like the nurture provided by a mother and the strength provided by a father.

In his appeal, Paul writes, "You are witnesses, and so is

God, how devoutly and uprightly and blamelessly we behaved toward you believers" (verse 10). In other words, Paul and his ministry partners conducted themselves with integrity. A father is to set the standard of integrity for his family.

The term translated "devoutly" means "piously, holy." It has to do with your life before God. Paul said he carried out his duty as God wanted him to. The word "uprightly" refers to how you respond to the law of God in your relationships with God and people. And "blamelessly" speaks of your reputation before other people. A father is to be upright and blameless.

Holy integrity is the key to producing spiritually strong children. Godly fathers must be steadfastly committed to living devoutly, uprightly, and blamelessly. When you demonstrate integrity, moral courage, and strength of conviction, you give your children the opportunity to emulate those same character qualities. It all starts by setting a pattern for your children and modeling integrity.

The Elements of a Father's Leadership

Paul continues, "You know how we were exhorting and encouraging and imploring each one of you as a father would his own children" (verse 11).

A Father Exhorts by Giving Instruction

The term translated "exhorting" refers to coming alongside someone, or moving someone toward a specific line of conduct. A father comes alongside his children and guides them toward appropriate behavior. Such personal instruction is to be done through exhortation or passionate urging.

A Father Encourages Through Motivation

A father is also to be "encouraging" his children. It's at this point that instruction turns into motivation. A father is to appeal to his children's emotions and will and move them to make the right choices. He lets them know the way will be hard, and urges them to hang in there and keep doing what is right. A godly father looks for ways to motivate his children toward walking on the right path in life.

A Father Implores Through Witnessing

Finally, a father is to commit to "imploring" his children. The Greek term used here is *marturomenoi*, which means "testifying" or "witnessing." In other words, a father is to say to his children, "Can I tell you something? I'm a personal witness to the fact that if you keep following a certain path, this is what's going to happen. I don't want you to fall into the same hole I did."

As a father, you're to watch out for your children's welfare. You have a solemn responsibility to warn them that, when they deviate from God's prescribed course of conduct, there will be serious consequences. If for some reason your children don't listen, that's where discipline comes in.

These are among the ways a father is to lead his children—by exhorting them, encouraging them, and imploring them. This means coming alongside each of them personally and teaching them God's pattern for conduct. It means encouraging them to be faithful when the choices are hard. And it means warning them that there are consequences when they do wrong—consequences that might include discipline. That is all part of the leadership you are to provide in the home.

The Objective of a Father's Leadership

What is the goal of exhorting, encouraging, and imploring your children? "So that [they] would walk in a manner worthy of the God who calls [them] into His own kingdom and glory" (1 Thessalonians 2:12). A father has his eyes on the end product of his parenting. He wants to make sure that, in the long term,

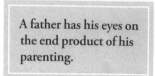

A father has his eyes on the end product of his parenting.

his children are living according to God's standards. His goal is to bring his children up toward spiritual maturity. In fact, he has God's future kingdom and glory in mind. He tells his children, "This is what lies ahead for those who follow God. In light of all that God has done for you, don't you think you ought to live the way God has called you to live?" A father lets his children know the kind of future that awaits them when they come to faith in Christ.

Making It All Happen

As a father, then, you are called to be strong and courageous. You are urged to live with conviction and not waver when opposition comes your way. You are to summon your courage from the assurance of God's presence, from knowing you are pursuing a just cause, and from the promise of God's sovereign power over all things. And you are to pass on your strength and courage by exhorting your children, encouraging them, and imploring them. As you do so, you will fulfill your obligation to ensure they walk upon—and stay upon—the path God has called them to.

That's an enormous responsibility. After reading all that, you may be asking yourself, "How can I possibly be sufficient to provide that kind of leadership?" The answer is that without God's empowerment, no man is sufficient. Where does our sufficiency lie? As Paul said of his apostleship, "Such confidence we have through Christ toward God. Not that we are adequate in ourselves to consider anything as coming from ourselves, but our adequacy is from God" (2 Corinthians 3:4-5). It's impossible to be an effective spiritual leader without God's grace. Here are some principles to keep in mind:

Realize Your Inadequacy

Fulfilling your role as the spiritual leader of your family starts by admitting your inadequacy and your full dependence upon God for help. As God told the apostle Paul in 2 Corinthians 12:9, "My grace is sufficient for you, for power is perfected in weakness." It's when you yield yourself fully to God that He can work through you and enable you to fulfill your divine duties as a dad.

Study the Word Intensely

In 2 Timothy 3:17, Paul talks about the "man of God" who is "adequate, equipped for every good work." What is it that equips such a man? You'll find the answer back in verse 16: "All Scripture is inspired by God and profitable for teaching, for reproof, for correction, for training in righteousness." If you are wondering what you should be doing as a father, the Bible will tell you. Study it, and you'll be equipped to lead your family.

Accept Suffering as Part of God's Tenderizing Process

First Peter 5:10 says, "After you have suffered for a little while, the God of all grace, who called you to His eternal glory in Christ, will Himself perfect, confirm, strengthen and establish you." God promises to perfect and strengthen you, to confirm and establish you. But it can't happen until you've suffered for a while. That is, God will use the problems and difficulties of life to shape and mold you toward spiritual maturity. As a Christian, there are things that suffering can accomplish in you that nothing else can. That, of course, will help you to become a better father.

Give Your Whole Life to Being the Leader Your Family Needs

In 1 Corinthians 9:24 Paul asks, "Do you not know that those who run in a race all run, but only one receives the prize? Run in such a way that you may win." He then adds, "I run in such a way...I box in such a way...I discipline my body...[so that I] will not be disqualified" (verses 26-27). In other words, put your heart, soul, mind, and strength toward excelling in the race. Give yourself completely to fulfilling your responsibilities as the spiritual leader of your family.

That's the kind of leader God wants. And it's the kind of leader your family needs.

Notes

1. Rich Gregory, "Real Men Love Their Wives: Lessons from the Life of Peter," in *Men of the Word*, ed. Nathan Busenitz (Eugene, OR: Harvest House, 2011), 126.

2. Weldon Hardenbrook, "Where's Dad?" in *Recovering Biblical Manhood and Womanhood*, John Piper and Wayne Grudem, eds. (Wheaton, IL: Crossway, 1991), 378-79.

3. C.H. Spurgeon, "A Glorious Church," sermon preached at the Metropolitan Tabernacle on May 7, 1865.

4. Martyn-Lloyd Jones, *Life in the Spirit in Marriage, Home and Work—An Exposition of Ephesians 5:18 to 6:9* (Grand Rapids: Baker, 1974), 301.

5. Neil Postman, *The Disappearance of Childhood* (New York: Delacorte Press, 1982).

6. Ibid., 134.

7. Ibid.

8. The issue of how to best discipline children is a matter of much controversy today, particularly in the area of whether it is appropriate for parents to spank their children. What constitutes biblical discipline? For more guidelines on this, see my article "Parenting in an Anti-Spanking Culture" at the Grace to You website, at http://www.gty .org/resources/articles/A216/Parenting-in-an-AntiSpanking-Culture.

9. Bryan Chapell, *Ephesians* (Phillipsburg, NJ: P&R Publishing, 2009), 319.

10. Ted Tripp, *Shepherding a Child's Heart* (Wapwallopen, PA: Shepherd Press, 1995), 39.

11. J.C. Ryle, *Wheat or Chaff?* (New York: Robert Carter, 1853), 233.

12. Philip Graham Ryken, *Luke,* vol. 2 (Phillipsburg, NJ: P&R Publishing, 2009), 146.

13. Elyse Fitzpatrick and Jim Newheiser, *When Good Kids Make Bad Choices* (Eugene, OR: Harvest House, 2005); Rick Horne, *Get Offa My Case! Godly Parenting of an Angry Teen* (Wapwallopen, PA: Shepherd Press, 2012).

14. John Gill, *A Body of Practical Divinity,* 2 vols. (London: Thomas Tegg, 1839), 2:519.